# CASKETS FROM COSTCO

KELLY WILSON

Cover Design by Troy Johnson
Edited by Wendy Garfinkle

Previously published as *Caskets From Costco*
Booklocker 2014

PRINT ISBN 978-0-9976208-0-1
EPUB ISBN 978-0-9976208-1-8
Library of Congress Control Number: 2015951541

# TABLE OF CONTENTS

# ACKNOWLEDGMENTS

I consider this the equivalent of my Oscar speech, and I have a lot of people to thank. Plus, I have the luxury of not being played off the stage.

I'm blessed with an incredible support system. My husband, Jeff, has listened to several years of my neurotic-writer ramblings and has talked me down countless times when I've wanted to quit. He's taken over the drudgeries of life in order to give me the gift of time so I can finish this book. He has supported me without fail every step of the way in this unpredictable career path. He is a gift. I love him…more than he'll ever know (this is our private joke, by the way, even though it's true).

My children have made me a better person. When Aaron was born, I couldn't process that hot mess without writing about it. I ended up embracing the reality that I'm a writer. With Noah, I learned to cling to the idea that I'm funny. So without them, who knows who I'd be?

I also thank Charlotte Kammer, Tae-ja Griggs, and Christine Draper for asking about and listening to hours upon hours of my grief experiences and encouraging my healing – this is only one aspect of how you have loved me through the years. You're the best friends in the world, and I look forward to being "Golden Girls" with you.

My Southeastside Stories ladies – Kathleen King, Jone Rush-MacCulloch, Susan Boase, and Lisa Mills – what would I do without you? I'm blessed by your friendship, your writing talent, your input, your critiques, your wine, and your snacks. Thank you for believing in this project and for listening to my whining, encouraging me the whole way, and not allowing me to burn this manuscript in my backyard.

Immense thanks to Jen Violi, who helped smooth out the rough edges through mad revising and editing skills. I couldn't have finished this project without you.

Thank you to Jamie Young for your constant help and talent with website stuff. You save me sanity and many hours of frustration.

Thanks also to Heidi Feigenbaum, Bryan Williams,, Sarah Clark, Alvin Nakamura, and Darbi Johnson. You know what you did.

# AUTHOR'S NOTE

It's important to remember that while tackling the serious, spiraling nature of the grief cycle, this book is also meant to be funny. And because it's a story about my experiences dealing with both humor and grief, there was no way to avoid writing about people who appeared in various times and places in my life. Without the friends and family contained in the pages of this book, my grief journey would've been quite boring indeed.

Aside from my husband and children (who don't have a choice in the matter), nobody in this book retains their real name. I've either fashioned fake names or have asked those who appear in this book what names they would like to be called.

This is why it would appear that some of my friends have what are known as "bar names." These are pseudonyms given out during sojourns to the local pub to avoid the awkward situation of a) being recognized, or b) being found in the future by someone you'd rather leave in dim memory.

For example, a friend of mine gave me my "bar name," which is Ivana Everwood. Considering the raging hormones I've experienced and demonstrated since I hit my 30th birthday, this is an accurate name, although not one I felt compelled to use in this work.

*This book is dedicated to children and adults who have experienced unspeakable trauma.*

*You are Survivors with a capital S.*

# DISCLAIMER

This book details the author's personal experiences with and opinions about abuse, grief and loss. The author is not a healthcare provider.

The author and publisher are providing this book and its contents on an "as is" basis and make no representations or warranties of any kind with respect to this book or its contents. The author and publisher disclaim all such representations and warranties, including for example, warranties of merchantability and healthcare for a particular purpose. In addition, the author and publisher do not represent or warrant that the information accessible via this book is accurate, complete or current.

The statements made about products and services have not been evaluated by the U.S. Food and Drug Administration. They are not intended to diagnose, treat, cure, or prevent any condition or disease. Please consult with your own physician or healthcare specialist regarding the suggestions and recommendations made in this book.

Except as specifically stated in this book, neither the author or publisher, nor any authors, contributors, or other representatives will be liable for damages arising out of or in connection with the use of this book. This is a comprehensive limitation of liability that applies to all damages of any kind, including (without limitation) compensatory; direct, indirect or consequential damages; loss of data, income or profit; loss of or damage to property and claims of third parties.

This book is not intended as a substitute for consultation with a licensed healthcare practitioner, such as your physician. Before you begin any healthcare program, or change your lifestyle in any way, consult your physician or other licensed healthcare practitioner to ensure that you are in good health and that the examples contained in this book will not harm you.

This book provides content related to topics physical and/or mental health issues. As such, use of this book implies your acceptance of this disclaimer.

*Grief never ends, but it changes. It's a passage, not a place to stay. Grief is not a sign of weakness, nor a lack of faith. It is the price of love.*

~Author Unknown

# SECTION ONE

## The Flipped Switch

# 1

## Grief Journey: GPS Not Required

**I GET LOST USING A GPS.**

Don't get me wrong, I use a GPS when I'm trying to find my way, but it's more of a security blanket than anything else. It doesn't necessarily offer the security of correct directions, but the GPS fits snugly into my palm as I carry it around, just in case.

Why carry a GPS if it's so useless? Because I have no sense of direction. I understand the compass rose in theory, but my navigational skills consist of, "Head down that one road that goes by the Beaver's Inn and turn left and then right at the crooked tree. What do you mean is that north or south? I don't know, it's left; just do it."

I get lost. A lot.

So I carry around the GPS and occasionally feel the need to turn it on and consult a map. But I've found through my many years of getting lost that even though there's a map in front of me, this doesn't guarantee that I'll get from Point A to Point B without detours or diversions.

Kind of like the grief process.

When I was in college, I learned that there are five stages in order to appropriately process grief. They're locked in my memory as the acronym "DABDA," which stands for Denial, Anger, Bargaining, Depression, and Acceptance, terms coined by Elizabeth Kubler-Ross.

I bought into this concept with my whole being, interpreting the process as set-in-stone directions for grieving – a Grief Positioning System, if you will. I was going to navigate quickly and efficiently through my past trauma, happily leaving it behind me. There was nothing I wanted to do more than "Get Over IT," whatever IT happened to be.

I wrote out my list of difficult experiences from which I wanted to be free, greatly anticipating the person I would become once my checklist of grief was completed.

That was over twenty years ago. Currently, none of the items are crossed off.

I had missed a fundamental principle: While there may be a Grief Positioning System with directions for navigation, there are often several ways to get from Point A to Point B.

For a while, I was angry with the stages of grief theory and claimed it was fundamentally flawed as a Grief Positioning System, blaming it and Kubler-Ross for leading me astray. As usual, though, my misunderstanding of her work was the result of what we call in the technological world, "Operator Error," like when the printer isn't printing and I think something's wrong with it, but it's actually because I didn't turn the blasted thing on.

Upon further reflection on the work of Kubler-Ross (after reading it again), I've decided that I may have been a little zealous about this set-in-stone linear map regarding the stages of grief.

But this led to the liberating realization that while stages of grief provide some helpful direction, a Grief Positioning System isn't required to navigate this particular kind of journey.

This is my messy, circular, spiraling-up-and-down grief journey navigated with large doses of humor.

And without a map.

## Casket Questions

I discovered that Costco sells caskets in October 2009. Have you ever seen a collection of caskets in the middle of a Costco warehouse? I haven't, and I wish they'd carry them in the store instead of only online. I imagine a large circle of caskets set up where the tables of clothing usually stand, arranged head to toe with room on both sides for browsing and comparing. To make good use of this space, some caskets could hold collections of smaller products or trays of food samples.

Many times, vendors come into Costco and set up tables to sell unique goods and services. Why not a series specializing in caskets and wakes along cultural themes? The Irish wake could feature bottles of Irish Cream and potatoes, and Greek Week could offer samples of Feta cheese and gyros made in the café with some shots of ouzo. Envision for a moment the week preceding Halloween, where employees dressed as ghosts and ghouls could pop out, thrilling shoppers who like to buy in bulk.

I imagine some people would find this distasteful, and that's why they don't do it.

My counselor Hannah told me about Costco caskets when my husband needed an MRI for a long-suffering back issue. I was convinced that the MRI would find a tumor the size of a tennis ball pressing on his spinal cord or something equally ominous.

"So, what you do NOT need to do is start shopping for caskets," Hannah said.

I nodded, sniffling, wiping my eyes with a crumpled tissue. I sat hunched in the black leather chair in one corner of Hannah's office, snuggled under a heavy fleece blanket. It was evening, the lights low, the scent of a Yankee Vanilla Candle – no other brand was at all acceptable to Hannah – wafting through the air.

Hannah sat across from me, curled into the black leather couch, also under a blanket. Her brown, wavy hair escaped from the casual bun gathered on the back of her head.

"Although you could," she continued, "on Costco-dot-com." She flashed an impish grin and adjusted her glasses.

I smirked. "Right."

"No, you can," Hannah insisted. "I promise."

"What category is it under?" I asked. "Furniture?"

"Caskets."

I threw my head back and guffawed.

"Yep," Hannah continued. "There's a tab across the top of the webpage. I didn't believe it, so I clicked it. Consequently, my husband had all kinds of questions."

I giggled. "Like what?"

"Do they deliver? To your house or to the store? Is there any assembly required? Can you choose the lining?"

"Oh, STOP!" I said. "He did not."

"He did! He went on for fifteen minutes! 'Do you have to pay taxes? Is there a double warranty like when you buy electronics? Does it come in a box? Will they help you get it out to your car?'"

I thrashed around in the chair, shoulders shaking. "I can't take it," I said.Hannah uncurled from under the blanket, tossing it aside and reaching for her slip-on shoes while my laughter subsided. When she put on her shoes, I knew that our time was almost up. She perched on the edge of the couch, and her eyes met mine.

"The point is," she said, "that although you could shop for caskets, you don't need to. There are a few steps before that."

"Like what?" I smiled. The laughter had alleviated the fear somewhat.

"Like getting information. Let's just see what the MRI says."

I nodded. "I can do that." I wiped the tears from my face with a crumpled tissue. "I'm scared, though."

"Yep," Hannah said with a nod. "But you have so much strength. There's so much about you that's strong and healthy, you just don't see it because you live in your own skin. Your fear is actually a sign of that strength."

I started crying again, but this time for a totally different reason besides fear for my husband. I rejoiced for a moment that my fear wasn't a sign of weakness but of strength. It gave me hope, realizing that all of the loss and grief I'd experienced had built up my emotional muscles, and they weren't going to let me down now.

# 2

## After Death Nuts and Bolts

### 6-6-6 (As In, June 6, 2006)

**JIM HADN'T ALWAYS** been a religious man.

He hadn't always been my father-in-law either. His youngest son, Jeff, and I began dating in high school after meeting on the band bus on the way to a football game. Jeff and I talked about farting, which turned out to be a talent passed down from Jim to both Jeff and his older brother Steve and, later, the grandchildren.

Sometimes it's impossible to quantify the value of a strong family heritage.

The legacy passed down from Jim extended to physical appearance. Both Jeff and Steve were tall, dark, and handsome with hazel eyes but a tendency toward body hair that could be fashioned into suits, including a unibrow. And while Jim successfully sported a full-on broom-style mustache, this wasn't something that either of his kids could ever carry off.

Jim was delightfully mischievous, much like Jeff. I discovered this early in our relationship as a freshman in high school. Jeff and I had only been dating a short time when Jim and Evelyn, Jeff's mom, treated us all to dinner.

We sat at a table at Skipper's during a Friday night all-you-can-eat fish extravaganza. Our short conversations were punctuated by trips for refills of fish, fries, chowder, and soda.

"So, how's school going?" Jim asked as I returned to the table after one of these trips. He grinned at me, his face flushed all the way up to his hairline, which had receded almost to the back of his head. There was no comb-over, just a cul-de-sac head of hair.

"It's good," I said, describing various assignments and activities.

I grabbed my soda, bringing the straw close to my mouth but not taking a sip.

"OH!" I said. "I wanted to tell you about the Sadie Hawkins dance coming up."

As I placed my soda back on the table to talk about this important development, I noticed Jim, Evelyn, and Jeff struggling to stifle giggles and eat their fish without choking. Evelyn carefully adjusted her glasses, strategically covering her face as her dark hair was carefully styled and out of the way.

Done talking, I ignored them, taking a bite of fish slathered in tartar sauce. I picked up my soda, once again bringing the straw to my mouth.

They stared at me while I sipped. The rank taste of diet soda mixed with malt vinegar assaulted my tongue.

"Agh! What is this?" I yelled, spraying soda over the top of the table.

They erupted in laughter, Jim shaking and wheezing, clutching the bottle of malt vinegar. Clearly he'd been the one to doctor my soda.

Therefore, I was always a bit careful when it came to taking a meal with them after that. Jeff often invited me to dinner at his house, where everyone sat at the table and there was always a bowl of rolls or bread of some kind, which to me was heaven on earth.

But, because Jeff and I were involved in youth group, it was during these meals that Jim would quiz us with a measure of bitterness about why God let babies die and similar questions that generally puzzle theologians.

By the time I was in college, Jim had become a Christian, getting baptized and serving in the same local church that Jeff and I had attended. His mischievous streak didn't end once he became a Christian, however. I believe it was at the dinner table one night when he coined the term "Funbags," pointing to Evelyn's chest.

*   *   *

I was sure that Jim was getting a kick out of the date on June 6, 2006. It had gotten a lot of media attention, something about how the 6-6-(0)6 made the sign of the devil, or maybe it was just that the date, month, and year were all the same number.

That's not why I remember that particular date, however.

"There was an accident. Jim was driving the school bus," Steve said. "He's at the hospital. You need to come right now."

I hung up the phone, scrambling, throwing clothes in duffel bags and trying to get a hold of Jeff, still at work, confused about how to tell him that his dad was in the hospital two hours away.

"Hello?" he answered his cell phone.

"Hi," I said. "We have to leave. We have to leave now."

"Wait. What are you talking about?" he asked.

I took a deep breath. Just the facts, I thought. "Your dad's been in an accident. He's in the hospital, and we have to go up there."

"I'm coming home."

By the time he arrived home, I had duffel bags packed and sitting by the front door. The kids were eating at the table, otherwise ready to go. Amidst a flurry of phone calls to make work arrangements and notify friends, we loaded Jeff's car and were on the road within ten minutes.

Once on the freeway, the silence descended. "What happened?" he asked.

"I don't know."

The road stretched out in front of us, full of questions but empty of answers.

About an hour into our drive, Jeff's cell phone rang. I could tell from his side of the conversation that we no longer needed to hurry.

"They tried to keep him alive until we got there," Jeff said. "It looks like a car hit his bus, and while he was filling out the paperwork for the police, he had a heart attack."

I nodded, clasping my heads together to try and warm them up.

"My mom said we can see him when we get there."

"I don't know about that," I said.

About an hour later, sitting in the hospital waiting room, I still wasn't sure. And it was almost my turn.

Jeff and Evelyn disappeared behind the door of the ICU, buzzed open from the other side. When they returned ten minutes later, I surrendered the kids to Evelyn.

"Ready?" Jeff asked.

I nodded, sick to my stomach. I didn't want to go in there, but I didn't not want to go either. The door buzzed, and Jeff held it open for me.

The fluorescent lights reflected off the sterile glass walls that separated rooms in the ICU. Nurses at their station looked up, recognized Jeff, and returned to their work.

Jeff led me around a corner and into Jim's room.

The door slid silently open. We pushed the curtain back and found Jim lying on the hospital bed in a gown. His eyes were closed and his mouth was open, his skin chalky and his hair grayer than I'd ever seen it.

You don't usually see people lying with mouths open unless they're sleeping or perhaps snoring, chests rising and falling with each breath. But there was no breath and his bony chest protruded up, the rest of his body pressed down into the bed. His fingertips had started to turn black.

"He's cold," Jeff said. He rubbed Jim's arm and shoulder.

I recoiled, not understanding how Jeff could touch him. Tears sat, stubborn, behind my eyes.

I felt the chill of death and the shell that once held a soul; at the same time I felt the sacredness of this moment, the holiness of the spirit freed from its body and moving on.

*     *     *

Afterward, Steve and his family met us at Evelyn's house. After the kids were in bed, the adults sat around the dining room table in awkward silence.

We participated in self-conscious conversation about arrangements – who would be involved in different tasks, what would happen to Jim's body, when would the obituary be written, where the funeral would take place – like the five w's of death. One of us would ask a question, my mother-in-law Evelyn would answer it, and we'd look at each other awkwardly for a few seconds before the next halting question.

Jim had decided he wanted to be cremated. Just an FYI, cremation is the most budget-friendly if you're stuck choosing between it and burial. I've since found out that the Neptune Society has branches in various cities throughout the country, and the cost for your basic cremation runs about $50 to $60.

The Neptune Society has a seemingly unnecessary measure of mystery concerning their cremation services. There's no signage or other identifying clues as to what they're doing at each particular location. Are they trying to save money on advertising? Are they trying to hide their presence from the neighbors? Why did they choose the name "Neptune," and is it a secret society? Why not a name that represents fire, like "Mars," instead of using the name of the Greek god of the ocean?

I had many questions, all inappropriate for this particular meeting.I don't remember that anyone cried around my mother-in-law's table during this discussion. But then again, I'm not one to cry in stressful or difficult situations, so this didn't seem odd. Instead, I make jokes.

They don't always go over very well.

The discussion faded into silence. Staring at the swirling wood grain of the table, I said to nobody in particular, "I think Jim would've gotten a kick out of dying on 6-6-(0)6."

Hearing no response, I looked up and found all eyes focused on me. Facial expressions ranged from blank to frowning, except for my husband. Jeff nodded slightly, and a flicker of a smile played around the corners of his mouth.

Too soon, I thought.

## Full Access?

The morning after Jim's death, as I dried off after my shower, I wondered to what extent, if at all, Jim was...around.

Could he look down on us? Could he be with us, not seen or sensed, but able to observe? Was he able to blip in and out, like the cameras of a reality TV show, observing us at random moments, with access to everything?

Most importantly at this moment, could he possibly see me naked? I looked around the bathroom, and I wanted to ask, "Are you here?" I also wanted to say, "Avert what passes for your eyes at this point." But I didn't.

The next day, I shared my thoughts with Bobbi Cumberbun, a good friend who came to hang out during the days after Jim's death.

Bobbi is the youngest of four children. She's been known to sign the "i" with a heart over it. I'm the older of two children, and my name is Kelly with a "y." No heart. Bobbi is miniature and petite. I'm gangly with a large frame and plain features, easily lost in a crowd.

Bobbi and I lived in the same town, went to the same church, and attended the same college. Opposite in many ways, we made an odd pair, but our similarities have become more obvious throughout the years.

Bobbi's mom became ill with flu symptoms on a Saturday in January five years before Jim's death. Diagnosed with a rare blood disease, she was admitted into the hospital in May and died later that month.

If there's something you want to talk about concerning death and grief, Bobbi's your girl.

She understood exactly what I meant about wondering if Jim was hanging around. "Don't you remember Mary Jo and the Nut Shack?" she asked.

"What are you talking about?" I asked.

Bobbi was sixteen when she worked at the Nut Shack; Mary Jo, then twenty-two, was a manager of sorts. One night they told their parents (Mary Jo still lived with her mother) that they were spending the night at each other's houses.

Instead, Mary Jo rented them a hotel room, where they got wasted on cheap light beer.

"Light beer?" I asked. "Can you really get drunk from light beer?"

Bobbi nodded. "And wine coolers."

The morning after her mother's death, Bobbi woke up, marched into her father's room, and confessed every detail of that night with Mary Jo even though it'd happened several years earlier.

"Why?" I asked."Same thing you were talking about," she said. "I didn't want to take the chance that he was finding out from Mom in some dream."

I had to agree.

I just really hoped that Jim – or any other person transitioning into the afterlife – couldn't see me naked.

## Androgynous Funeral

A breeze wafted through the high-ceilinged room. Sun reflected on the hardwood floors. Blue tablecloths and a variety of delicious food covered long tables.

My father-in-law's Gathering, and I didn't know anybody there besides my family members. I say 'Gathering' because it wasn't really a funeral or memorial service, but everyone was there because someone had died.

This event refused to commit.

Even though my stomach ached from stress, I scooped pasta salad and marinated artichoke hearts onto my plate. Strangers gathered at tables around the room, consuming pre-made deli sandwiches and fruit and drinking cans of soda.

At one point, someone started the video my brother-in-law had made for the occasion. It included photos spanning Jim's life, set to a backdrop of the country music he preferred. The last pictures were of Jim driving away in his school bus, and my breath hitched in my chest.

The music faded, and the screen went dark. Someone turned off the TV, and I surveyed the faces in the room. Reflective. Thoughtful. Totally dry. The attendees sighed and went back to eating and chatting.

Conversation and laughter intertwined, echoing in the high-ceilinged room and bouncing around the inside of my head. Forks scraped against plates, scooping hunks of potato salad, chocolate cake, and marinated vegetables into wide, eager mouths. A middle-aged lady with broccoli stuck in her yellowed teeth laughed with a younger woman, while a man in a leather jacket lounged nearby, a plate of crumbs in front of him.

As they slurped and chewed, I thought to myself, who are these people?

It turned out that they were mostly friends of my brother- and sister-in-law, basically there to show support. Consequently, my husband spent the entire afternoon being introduced to people he didn't know.

On a good day, I'm not interested in meeting people I don't know. This wasn't a good day.

Therefore, I abandoned my plate and hunkered down in the bathroom.

One of those fancy bathrooms, this large room had no stalls, just the toilet and a sink and flowered décor adorning every inch of available wall and counter space. After taking advantage of the opportunity to empty my bladder then hunting through the cabinet under the sink just for kicks, I didn't have anything to do. These were the days before everyone carried a smartphone and could play Words With Friends while on the toilet.

I had a lot of time to think.

This Gathering wasn't really a Funeral, but it wasn't a Non-funeral either. It was an Androgynous Funeral.

I know a little bit about androgyny. My nickname was "Pat" in high school, in honor of the androgynous character played by Julia Sweeney on *Saturday Night Live* in the mid-1990s.

The reasons for this nickname were clear:

- My first name – Kelly – can be a boy's or girl's name.
- I had shorter hair.
- My clothes were always baggy, and appropriate for either boys or girls.
- I wasn't a big fan of make-up or hair products.

And I suppose from the back, there was no way to tell if I was male or female.

I eventually grew out of the nickname – birthing kids and breastfeeding helped. But I still hear it every once in a while from old friends of mine. It reminds me that I come from somewhere specific and that I've known people for a number of years. As an Army Brat before that, I'd come from everywhere and nowhere because we moved around so often. And the nickname helped ground me during those years when my family imploded and I didn't quite know where I would land.

For me, this nickname was – and continues to be – a badge of honor. It proved that I belonged, and for a kid who had been without a community, this was a great feeling.

While I took cover in the bathroom, I explored all of the ways this funeral could be considered Androgynous. First, consider the elements of a Funeral:

- Takes place shortly after a person dies
- There's a body in a box
- People dress up
- Music and pictures are shown, and/or a slideshow
- People weep
- Story-telling and laughter about the person and his/her life
- Religious justification or silence
- A time for food and drinks

A true Non-funeral would be like a party, with the following characteristics:

- Everyone is alive, and there's no body in a box
- People dress up
- There's music and dancing, possibly karaoke
- People taking photos
- The absence of routine religious symbols or traditions
- Food and drinks with and without alcohol

I plotted it all out on a piece of paper: Jim's gathering had elements of the Funeral and the Non-funeral.

| Funeral | Non-funeral |
|---|---|
| A death had occurred | No body in a box |
| People dressed up | No crying |
| A slideshow | No story-telling |
| Food | Absence of religious elements |

This mix of the Funeral and the Non-funeral led to feelings of overwhelming confusion. The consequence of attending an Androgynous Funeral is that I really had no clue how I was supposed to behave in the situation. Now, at last, I have the following guidelines:

At a Funeral, I tell stories, laugh, and remember. At a Non-funeral, I eat, laugh, and have fun.

At an Androgynous Funeral, I hide in the bathroom. Throughout my varied and intimate experiences with grief, I wondered if there would simply come a day when I couldn't take anymore. I imagined that at the beginning of the next crisis, my brain would finally shout "THAT'S IT!" I would instantly go from survival mode to certifiably insane, living as hermit in a cave in central Montana (if indeed there are caves in that part of the United States), or at least as part of a militia in a ramshackle cabin deep in the woods.

It turns out that Jim's death was the catalyst that flipped that switch in my brain. But I didn't immediately head for Montana. Instead, I decided to give counseling a try.

# 3

## Counseling or a Montana Cave

### *Making the Appointment*

COUNSELING WASN'T a new concept for me – in college, counseling was free, and I've always loved a bargain. During those appointments, I learned that when I was around ten years old, my brain assumed depression was the way to cope with all of the dysfunction and abuse happening around me.

And, because I subscribed to the whole idea that I'd "gotten over" depression by going to counseling during my college years, it seemed that I'd prematurely crossed "dealing with depression" off my list of things to do.

My experience birthing Aaron was so traumatic that the seeds for post-partum depression were firmly planted. Noah's birth was also an ordeal, allowing those post-partum depression seeds to germinate in ground already fertile with past trauma.

Jim's death was just the sunlight and water in this metaphor that brought the depression to full growth.

Getting out of bed wasn't an issue for me; in fact, I was quite determined each morning that it was going to be a good day, that today I wouldn't cry.

By noon, I would be in tears. The process was exhausting.

It was while I was teaching my class of fourth graders that I realized something might be amiss. Shortly before noon, one of the students raised his hand in the midst of the quiet classroom of industrious learners. "Hey, what's up?" I asked from the aptly named kidney table where I sat.

"Aren't we going to go to lunch?" he asked.

I stared at the clock, horrified. It was fully ten minutes after lunch had started. This doesn't sound like a lot of time, but it cuts considerably into a lunch period that's only about twenty-two minutes long to begin with.

What frightened me was that I hadn't lost track of time or made a simple mistake. I'd completely forgotten about lunch because I simply wasn't functioning. If I couldn't even keep track of lunch time for myself and a classroom of kids, what else was I missing?

And I didn't know what to do about it.

I waited until I had apologized profusely and taken the kids to the cafeteria before allowing the tears to roll down my face. Hunkered down in a closet in the main office, I called a friend of mine, who gave me two choices: find a counselor myself or she would find one for me.

After a bit of research, I discovered that my employer provided a service to help find counselors. I even had insurance to help pay for it!

Finding a counselor appeared to be an easy, painless way to spend ten of my valuable minutes on this earth. All of the information I needed was on the web. A trip to my Montana cave wouldn't be necessary.

I blocked out time one afternoon to sit at the dining room table, laptop opened in front of me, and the phone clutched in my sweaty ham-hock of a palm.

Ten minutes turned into one hour, which turned into two. After three websites, two phone numbers, one voicemail with a litany of staff and extensions ("Dr. T. Wolfe, two-oh-one), and one faulty password, I stood on the verge of making an appointment or of simply buying a flask and calling it good.

"What's your subscriber number?" the receptionist asked.

"Like, for insurance?" I asked. We'd talked so much already that I knew her particular shade of lipstick and how many kids she had.

"Yes. We can't make an appointment without that information," she said.

All I had was a website where I'd looked up my benefits, which was a different company altogether from my health insurance company. Totally separate. Not linked in any way.

Did I mention that I was depressed?

This whole process of finding help actually wasn't helping. I opened a new window in my web browser to look up plane tickets to Montana.

After agreeing to call the receptionist back, I called my insurance company and explained my situation.

"Is the counselor approved through our system?"

"Yes, I looked her up on your website," I said.

"Why are you seeing the counselor?"

"Grief counseling."

"Do you have an appointment?" she asked.

"No, I'm trying to make one now, but I need some insurance information."

"Oh, well, we usually give an authorization number after an appointment is set."

"Riiiight," I said. "I'm depressed."

She gave me the authorization number. I had one final call to make, either the travel agent or the receptionist at my soon-to-be counselor's office.

I chose the receptionist. Made the appointment. Finally.

Thank God.

## Medication

My counselor's name was Hannah. I felt afraid to meet her. Maybe we wouldn't connect, or I would tell her about my experiences and she would think they were no big deal.

We sat across from each other on black leather furniture, stark against the white walls and tall windows that let in a generous amount of daylight. Stuffed animals sat around the room, strategically placed and promising comfort.

A solitary dream catcher adorned one wall, perfectly centered and, at less than a foot in length, odd in its simplicity because there was no other artwork. No photos, no Ansel Adams prints, no inspirational quotes – just the dream catcher.

Years later, I would find out that she'd previously had artwork on the walls in addition to the dream catcher, but her boss told her that the dream catcher would offend people and that she needed to take it down. Instead, she took everything down except the dream catcher.

That action has, to the present day, offended absolutely nobody. Not one person. Except maybe her boss.

"Have you considered taking antidepressants?" Hannah asked about a half hour into our first appointment.

"I'm certainly not against it," I said, wiping tears from my eyes.

"Well, think about this for a minute," she said. "It would be enough to have your husband and you working, two small children, and run a household."

"Okay."

"Then factor in your husband's ADHD, all of the events from the last four years, and your history of abuse."

"Yeah?"

"That's a shitload. For anyone. And I'm not into suffering."

I nodded, thinking about the stash of antidepressants I'd stopped taking a few months previous. They were in the drawer of my nightstand. And my prescription was still good.

I took one as soon as I got home.

*   *   *

After two days, my husband told me he already noticed a difference. I was no longer crying by noon every day, and I was actually engaging in conversations with Jeff and the boys.

I noticed a difference, too, but I wasn't sure if it was from the meds as much as finally dumping on someone who was being paid to help me out. Either way, I felt clearer and just a little bit lighter.

I'd thought of my response to her question about medication several times in the last two days – "I'm certainly not against it."

It didn't sound to me like I was for it, either.

When I have a headache, I don't analyze it. I don't ask the headache why I'm suffering with it at the moment or wonder how long it'll be there. I don't blame the headache for all of my troubles.

I don't think about the merits of ibuprofen, if I should take it or not, or question whether or not it will work.

I take a few ibuprofen and get on with life.

Not that depression can be boiled down to the simplicity of a headache, but every time I think about taking medication for depression, I think about how soon I can stop taking it.

My chest grows tight. Why do I have to deal with this again? When can I be done?

I resent the depression, hide from it, and don't admit that I'm suffering. I wonder about the prescribed meds, and I question if they'll really work or just mask my feelings and keep me from dealing with the "shitload" on my shoulders.

I recall first feeling depressed at the age of ten, sitting outside our apartment building after one of my parents' fights. Depression was like a heavy coat being placed around my brain, zipped up and protecting me from harmful elements but also hiding me from sunlight. Depression and I became fast friends.

In college, when I took advantage of the free on-campus counseling, I believed depression would be the friend I'd say goodbye to one day. It would fade out, like the good friend in high school who you call frequently after graduation and then only once in a while as years pass. We'd see each other during random school breaks, maybe at a reunion, and then eventually not at all.

After that first counseling appointment with Hannah, I retreated to one of my favorite places: my bed. I climbed in and covered my whole body with cool cotton and warm fleece and the weight of the heavy, soft comforter.

Jeff soon joined me. "How did it go?" he asked

"Fine." I buried my face in my pillow.

"Oh, come on, you're not getting away that easily," Jeff said, grabbing the blankets and pulling them off me.

I rolled over. "Fine!" I said. "But I want my blankets." Again securely covered, I filled him in about my appointment, Hannah, the dream catcher and shitload of stuff, and the medication.

"Medication itself isn't what bothers me," I said. "If I had diabetes, I would have no problem injecting myself with insulin. That's a physical illness. And I don't like that I feel funny about taking meds for depression."

I started to cry, just a few tears escaping down my cheeks.

"Which makes me think that depression is a mental illness," I said. "And I wonder who I could've been without it."

"I don't like that," he said. "That's saying that who you are now isn't valuable. And I don't believe that."

I cried harder at that.

I realized at that moment that depression and I will always be linked, tugging back and forth, like the drunken uncle who still gets invited to the family reunion even though everyone knows he's going to make a messy scene.

So it's not the medication that makes my chest grow tight, it's realizing that I'm mentally sick enough to need medicine.

Maybe I'll need to take meds for a long time, years instead of months.

Maybe forever.

# 4

# Order From Disorder

## *Does Not Play Well With Others*

**I'VE ALWAYS HAD** really good friends. Except one.

It wasn't until the Christmas season of 2006, after I'd been in counseling for a good five months, that I formally met my new friend: Post-traumatic stress disorder.

I've attempted for years to make fun of PTSD, which is a dangerous game. It's similar to poking fun at the largest, scariest bully at your school and assuming you won't get beat up.

For me, PTSD is like a good friend – I refer to "PTSD" as a "she." I'm not sexist; this is just how I see her in my mind's eye. A necessary girlfriend, but with chronic PMS. A temperamental – and even volatile – friend who does not play well with others and whom I dearly love.

It's a strange relationship.

I would like her to have a different name. The acronym "PTSD" is labor-intensive to say. People love their acronyms, especially in education – the RTI data for ELL is required for the IEP, which is then used during SST. When I taught elementary school, I used to collect acronyms and put them on Bingo Boards, one to a square, then mark off each one as it was said in a staff meeting. Five in a row was a BINGO, awarded with a cold, frosty beer (after work, of course).

A pastor at a church I once attended loved acronyms so much that one appeared in every sermon. Taking his lead, I proposed the new Young Marrieds Group be called "CULT" – Couples Under Leadership Training. Nobody went for it.

PTSD doesn't do her justice in a descriptive way either, like when women say that their "Aunt Flo" has come to visit – if you're female, you know exactly what this means. PTSD has been called a lot of names, like Battle Shock, Combat Exhaustion, Shell Shock, and Battle Fatigue. But these don't quite describe the kind of friend I'm talking about – one who will tell you that in fact your butt *does* look fat in those jeans or that the hair on your upper lip has grown in a little too thick.

Maybe a name based on actual symptoms would work. PTSD survivors experience a variety of the following:

- The memory or memories of a traumatic event (seems obvious, I know) involving intense fear and helplessness
- Intrusive recollections of the event, or elements associated with the event
- Distressing dreams, flashbacks, and hallucinations
- Triggers (sights, smells, sounds, calendar dates, or seasons of the year) that bring on psychological and/or physical distress

But how does all this information translate into real life?

For me, it's mostly about triggers. I can't go into a maternity ward without severe stress since both of my children and I almost died while staying in one. Certain smells or tones of voice will send me over the edge, along with feeling out of control, and there are many others.

My triggers occur during the holiday season more than any other time of the year. In December 2006, my husband and I found ourselves on a rare date night, free of our two young boys, ages four and one at the time. We decided to spend it doing one of the activities we loved best – wandering.

We arrived at Fred Meyer and browsed the fake display trees covered with dazzling colored lights and ornaments for sale. We held up ones we thought were particularly funny or tacky, like the Santa doing the hula while wearing sunglasses.

"Ugh," I said. "Santa."

"Why don't you like Santa?" Jeff asked.

I shrugged. We had this conversation every year. I'd never been able to explain it, just like I could never explain getting sick every Christmas.

We wandered separately for a while through the rows of shiny dishes and sparkling decorations. Jeff and I met up again, surrounded by fuzzy stockings and satiny tree skirts.

"Hey, look at this!" he said, turning around to face me.

Jeff's face was covered by a mask of white felt beard, eyebrows, and a Santa hat. His eyes peered out anonymously.

"Oh," I said. My stomach churned. I felt like I was falling, unable to breathe, reeling in murky water, drowning.

"What? What is it?"

"My dad," I said.

"Your dad?" Jeff removed the mask. His expression was a combination of confusion and concern. After all, I hadn't seen my biological father in over ten years.

"He used to dress up as Santa for Christmas."

"Oh." Jeff frowned. He watched me for a moment.

"Let's go home."

I wiped sweat from my forehead as we shuffled toward the car. I felt feverish, clammy, and panicked.

The next day, I explained what'd happened to Hannah.

She nodded with understanding. "That's very familiar."

"Really?"

"Oh, yeah. You had a trigger. You're dealing with a condition called Post-traumatic stress disorder."

"Oh." I felt relieved. My panic from the night before had a name. "Wait. What does that mean?"

"Well," Hannah said, "it means that you had – and will continue to have - an intense emotional reaction about past trauma."

"Oh. But past trauma is past, right?"

"Not necessarily."

"And that's the best name they can give this terrible experience?" I asked.

"Apparently."

So, yeah, Post-traumatic stress disorder needs a new name, one that adequately describes her. One of my suggestions is:

- Previous Overwhelming Trauma, Smothering Memories Overpowering Knowledge, Emotional Rollercoaster = POTSMOKER

That's better. Easy to remember and simple to say. But it does discriminate against actual pot smokers, because smoking pot doesn't necessarily mean you suffer from PTSD. Back to the drawing board.

What about other forms of figurative language to help explain PTSD symptoms through comparison in the form of a simile or metaphor?

- Scared Shitless Disorder (does this mean that when a trigger occurs, one actually poops one's pants right then? Or does it refer to constipation as a result of the trigger?)
- Panic Attack – I know this is an actual disorder, and I believe it's very aptly named. The idea that the panic is attacking you – brilliant!
- Deer in the Headlights Disorder – not a great acronym, but it's pretty descriptive.

Maybe describing it in a song would help. As a mother of young children, I understand the importance of song lyrics when helping kids learn and process information. Why couldn't there be a song that PTSD survivors could sing to help explain the disorder? "Memory" from the musical *Cats* seems like the most appropriate:

Memory
Terrifies in the moonlight
I can smile at the old days
I was non-triggered then
I remember the times of overwhelming fear
For me, the memories live again

Midnight
I have many distressful dreams
Reliving the trauma
I awake in a sweat
In the flashbacks
I'm right back in the thick of the shit
Sometimes I just want to forget

That's a good idea, but the song is a bit morose. Clear, but depressing.

I thought about inserting a couple of vowels in between the P, T, S and D – maybe PiTSaD – but it simply sounds like a melancholy armpit. That doesn't really serve as an explanation of the disorder in any way.

Maybe there are events or conditions that won't be mocked. Maybe they're too serious, like the scariest bully in school. Plus, I think PTSD would prefer I suffer through saying each consonant over and over. And even as unrelenting as she can be, I'm grateful to her friendship.

Without her, I wouldn't be able to heal.

*  *  *

As I occasionally peruse daytime TV, I sometimes land on commercials for depression research studies. Sad people stand in grainy black and white, staring into space, all blank eyes and frowns. They hold signs or speak directly into the camera, communicating messages like:

- "I can't get out of bed."
- "I have a hard time paying attention."
- "Nothing interests me."

These people kind of remind me of my children as whiny toddlers or teenagers (essentially the same developmentally, just radically different sizes).

To be completely honest, these commercials are, well, so…depressing.

And offensive to someone like me, who deals with depression on a regular basis. Just once, I would like to see someone on these commercials doing what I do when I'm depressed, for example:

- Binging on Lucky Charms, straight from the box.
- Writing angry emails to grocery stores when they don't accept my coupons.
- Using inappropriate language (except in front of the children).

- Considering punching the husband in the throat because his snoring is so loud in the middle of the night.
- Serving a non-organic and nutritionally defunct dinner, like Mac and Cheese from a box with a side of popcorn and apples.

It would be nice to be adequately represented.

There are so many layers to depression that include coping mechanisms and subgenres like anxiety and PTSD. Partly why I like PTSD as my bossy friend so much is that she provides clear signals to me that there's something happening in my brain. She gives me the chance to tune in, the time and space for my brain to hibernate, and the motivation to keep on a path of healing in order to manage those pesky triggers.

Without PTSD as my friend, I would swallow the idea that depression of all varieties is just about what's happening on those commercials instead of what it really can be, which is an opportunity for growth and healing.

If only I can remember that the next time I find myself halfway through a box of Lucky Charms.

## The Pooh Factor

I've always been a bit unnerved by the characters in Winnie the Pooh. I didn't realize it until I was pregnant with my oldest child, deep in the process of registering for baby necessities and nursery decorations.

With my mental list of wants and needs, I wandered the aisles, zapping bar codes with the inventory gun that automatically put items on our baby registry. As I selected bibs, bottles, blankets, diapers, bedding, and toys, I noticed that every single department had not one, but several Winnie the Pooh items.

Even the most unnecessary baby products, like a warmer that heats up baby wipes or a special pacifier holder, had Winnie the Pooh options. I began to see Winnie the Pooh characters everywhere I looked, whether they were present or not. I began to wonder whose face I would see if I looked in a mirror. It frightened me, and I shuddered as I shopped.

It wasn't until a counseling appointment in the summer of 2006 that I put my finger on just exactly what I didn't like about Winnie the Pooh and Company, and it even has a neat and tidy label – Learned Helplessness.

The characters of the Hundred Acre Wood are quite strange if you stop and think about them. There's Rabbit, who is a control freak teetering on the edge of Obsessive Compulsive Disorder. Roo and his mom live together in a tiny space, clearly enmeshed and possibly codependent. There's a needy piglet with a mysterious back story. Tigger, who specifically is not a tiger, appears to have serious impulse-control issues. Pooh's over in the corner, eating his feelings with the help of a honey jar, enabled by all of the others but at least self-medicating.

And then, there's Eeyore.

Tired, slow-moving, sad-sack Eeyore, his color a depressing combination of lavender and gray. The Victim. My least favorite character.

And that was me.

"It's called Learned Helplessness," Hannah told me in a tone that was both matter of fact and indisputable.

"What's that?" I asked. I grabbed a tissue and wiped my eyes, having just explained all of the ways I hadn't been happy in my relationships with others lately. I sat perched on the edge of the matching soft leather chair, unable to relax.

"Experience has taught you to do nothing because everything you do is useless."

"What do you mean, helpless?" I asked. "Or useless? I've done a lot with my life." Anger ignited in my chest and I radiated outward, drying my tears.

"Yes, you have," she said.

"I mean, I graduated high school, worked my way through college, became a teacher, am currently holding down a job and raising a family…how is any of that useless?" I spit the words out.

"All of that is true," she said.

"I'm not a victim!"

"Then why do you act like one?" Touché.

As I realized that she was right, my anger cooled, quickly replaced by confusion.

"I kind of get it," I said. "I understand with my gut, but not necessarily with my brain, if that makes any sense."

Hannah nodded. "An example, then," she said. "A lab rat is placed in a box where there's a small space to escape. Every time the rat heads for that space, he gets shocked. Pretty soon, he won't try to escape even if an entire wall is taken away – he's learned through experience that it's no use."

"That sounds incredibly cruel."

"It is," she said. "In reality, too. Think about situations involving domestic violence. Women learn to take the beating because they know that soon it'll be over and things will go back to 'normal'. Action isn't going to produce a different result."

I nodded, thinking about my childhood family, considering my current relationship challenges. I was tired of not really counting on anybody, not asking for help, not letting anybody get that close.

I'd always considered myself a Survivor rather than a Victim, or in the case of Winnie the Pooh, anyone but Eeyore. While Rabbit, Piglet, Kanga and Roo, Tigger, and Pooh represented a variety of mental eccentricities and personality quirks, they were, at least, action-oriented.

I believed I was a Survivor because I was alive after all of the traumatic episodes I'd endured in my lifetime up to that point. I had family and friends as well as a job that I'd wanted since I was twelve.

On paper, this looked good. But I was also severely depressed. At a loss for what I felt or needed, I was unable to verbally communicate with people on a deeper level, which is basically foundational for intimate relationships. I couldn't identify or communicate strong feelings with any kind of accuracy, allowing them to build until finally exploding in messy and confusing fights with family and friends.

I loved my job as a teacher, but I could barely function within it. And I won't mention trying to deal with my growing family obligations as the mother of two young children.

Or, as Eeyore aptly said: "Nobody tells me. Nobody keeps me informed. I make it 17 days come Friday since anybody spoke to me."[1]

In other words, sounding like what I'd been saying for years – Ignore me, I'm not important anyway.

"What are you thinking?" Hannah asked.

"Helpless," I said. "I don't like it. At all." All of the anger had drained, and I felt overwhelmed and tired. But my mind also felt clearer than it had in my entire life. For a brief moment, I glimpsed what my life could become if I could overcome living as Eeyore.

She nodded. "Learned Helplessness is just a name. Plus, you've already taken control."

## Dream #1

About a month after the Learned Helplessness conversation, I had the following dream:

*On a sunny afternoon, I walk up to a house I haven't seen before in Nevada, where my father reportedly now lives. It's a fairly new housing development, a nice one-story with a green lawn.*

*I ring the doorbell. I'm not afraid, only determined. When he answers the door, I raise the double-barrel shotgun that appears out of nowhere and aim it at his chest. I pull the trigger. He falls back in the entryway, dead.*

"What do you think about it?" Hannah asked.

"It's disturbing," I said.

"What happened with your dad?" Hannah asked. I shifted in the armchair. My eyes filled with tears.

"This is a safe place," she said. "You need to talk about it."

"I don't want to," I said. My chest felt full. I'd already dealt with this, right? I didn't want to talk about it anymore.

"Okay," she said. "But if there's a place you can talk about it – and I mean every detail – then it's here."

---

[1] Milne, A.A. *Winnie the Pooh*. United Kingdom: Methuen & Co. Ltd., 1926.

I sobbed, and she handed me a box of tissue. I pulled one after another, heaving tears until they subsided.

My chest felt lighter than it had in a long time.

"I can't start with that," I said. "It's easier to start from the end and circle back around."

"Whatever works." Hannah smiled at me.

"I know I need to talk about it," I said. "But I just can't get over that dream."

"Yes?" Hannah asked.

"You know, like, incredibly violent. It's a bit unnerving."

"And hopeful," she said. "You're gettin' your power back."

# SECTION TWO

## The Children

# 5

## The Voices in My Head Were Right

**BEFORE I HAD** my two children, I thought that I'd endured the absolute worst experiences that life could throw at me. I'd been through enough trauma to last my entire lifetime, and surely God and the universe would smile on me the rest of my days.

I was wrong.

### The Tiny Voice

I was sick for nine days before my OB/GYN, Dr. Al, told me that I had to give birth to my son. Which would've been fine, had it not been two and a half months before the actual due date.

It also might seem unnecessary that I'd been ill for nine whole days – to be fair, Dr. Al had gone on a well-deserved vacation that week. But I ask you, what good is an OB/GYN if he can't sense from miles away that something is terribly wrong?

My first clue that something was amiss began with a lone case of the vomits. At first, I was angry when I threw up at seven-and-a-half months pregnant. I work hard to avoid throwing up, and pregnancy had been no exception – I'd managed to avoid it even in the first trimester. The fact that my body betrayed me in this way woke a tiny voice in my head, whispering, *something might be wrong*. Being an apprentice hypochondriac, this isn't the first time I'd heard this particular voice. I generally ignore it.

But the voice wasn't the hypochondriac one that suggests that every cold is actually a tumor; it was the one that I'd heard first as a kid. It was the Danger Voice, and I'd obeyed it completely as a child before the logic of adulthood had set in with its own set of voices.

Since I was both cute and pregnant, I'd gotten a summer job as the Beer Cart Girl at a friend's golf course. The boss hired me partly because he knew that chances were good that I wouldn't be drinking the inventory while driving around.

Once the pain in my ribcage started, there was no way I could fulfill my highly-anticipated Beer Cart Girl commitment. I became pale and swollen. The pain traveled around my chest and back, sometimes stabbing while at other times taking on a pounding quality reminiscent of a headache.

At one point, I found myself bent over, hands clasped to my knees and unable to catch my breath. My knuckles went from pink to white. All I wanted was for the pain to stop.

Which it did, every once in a while. So, thinking they were gas cramps, I put off calling the doctor's office for a few days. Since I'd neither gone to medical school nor received any kind of medical degree, I had to be correct, right?

I noticed the pain occurred when I ate or drank, so I'd elected to do very little of either until the glorious Chinese buffet a few hours before, which had proven irresistible: crispy egg rolls filled with slimy vegetables and shrimp, tongue-tingling kung-pao chicken, sweet and sour everything, hot and sour soup, light fried dough rolled in crunchy sugar granules. Four 12-foot rows of steaming food nestled in stainless steel pans, waiting for me to eat it.

*Damn that Chinese buffet!* I thought as the now-familiar pain returned. I shifted, unable to get comfortable. Sighing, I rolled out of bed, resigning myself to a trip to the kitchen to retrieve my gas medicine. I would head off this siege. I flipped on my bedside lamp.

"Wha–?" Jeff started to ask, groggy with sleep.

"Just the gas again," I told him. He rolled back over, escaping the intrusive light.

*Something is definitely wrong,* the tiny voice nagged as I sipped water. It seemed to echo in the stillness of the kitchen. I popped the recommended dosage of gas medicine into my mouth, then one more for good measure.

No, nothing's wrong, I chided Danger Voice. It's just that stage of pregnancy – the part where I have to pee every three seconds and a teaspoon's worth comes out. The part where I can't get up from a chair inside of twenty minutes. The part where eating my weight at a Chinese buffet causes painful gas. It's not supposed to be a picnic; it's just been so easy for me so far that now it seems worse than it is.

*Something is wrong*, Danger Voice pestered, a little louder, a little stronger, a little more insistent.

Well, what if I call the doctor and nothing's wrong? I began to argue. What if I'm just some annoying, dramatic hypochondriac who's paranoid about GAS? And when will I call, Monday? What if the pain is gone? Then what will I say?

*Maybe you should call now.*

Now? It's practically the middle of the night. I'm not calling now.

And with that, I buried Danger Voice in my reasonable thoughts, and climbed the stairs back to bed.

*　*　*

*Call the doctor.*

The tiny Danger Voice was back only the tone had changed to demanding instead of persuasive. After another sleepless night, I was in no mood to argue.

Was it only a week ago that I had thrown up? Funny how I'd thought at the time it was the twenty-four hour flu.

I rolled over slowly towards the phone – it sat silently on Jeff's bedside table. He was in the shower, getting ready to go to a summer class to fulfill professional development requirements as a local high school band director.

"Thank you for calling our offices. Our hours are eight to five, Monday through Thursday, and eight to noon on Friday–"

I hung up, unwilling to listen or leave a message. I clicked on the television and watched the clock instead. I pleated the comforter and sheet between my restless fingers, smoothing it out and pleating it again and again. I redialed at 8:00 exactly. "Thank you for calling our–"

Maybe the clock is fast. I'll wait five more minutes. At 8:03 I called back and got a receptionist.

"I'd like to speak to a nurse, please," I spoke quietly. My stomach growled, but my fear of the pain was stronger than any complaint my stomach could lodge.

"Yes, may I help you?" a voice inquired.

I explained the last few days, my voice threatening to waver. I willed myself not to cry.

"There's been a nasty bug going around." The nurse paused for a moment, and I plucked at the pleated comforter. "But I think I'll have you come in anyway."

My heart soared as we finalized the appointment for that day. Someone would believe me! Someone would help me! The pain would soon be gone!

"Your doctor is on vacation until Wednesday," she said. "How about Dr. Stanford?"

I felt a brief disappointment, but nothing was going to keep me from the doctor's office. "Sure," I answered. "What time?"

\* \* \*

"We need a urine sample." The nurse handed me a clear plastic cup as I stepped off the scale, seven pounds lighter than my last appointment. I sighed and headed for the bathroom, wondering when I'd last peed.

Sitting on the toilet, I willed my bladder to fill, pleaded with it to produce a few drops for the expectant cup.

With relief, I managed to pee for three seconds. I carefully placed the cup on the edge of the sink.

Murky brown sludge swirled in the bottom of the cup. I stared, horrified. I'd never known urine to look like that. It was the color and consistency of pulpy apple cider. If I'd liked apple cider at all, I would no longer be a fan.

The nurse took it without comment and led me into an exam room. I was to receive a full exam to check my cervix. More digging around in my crotch. Fabulous.

There was a faint knock at the door, and Dr. Stanford entered for a pre-exam chat. Towering above me, his graying blond hair framed a strong face. Caring blue eyes surveyed me.

"So, Kelly," he started, flipping the top page of the chart, "you haven't been feeling so well lately?"

"Yeah," I mumbled, sitting on the paper-covered exam table.

"Hmm." He bit his lip with clean, straight teeth. "There's been a gastrointestinal bug making its way around, and it looks like you might be at the tail end of it. We're checking the baby and your cervix just to make sure, but there's really nothing you can do but wait it out."

I sighed heavily. Wait it out. I was too tired to argue. Too tired to cry.

"Should be soon," he said kindly. "I'll be right back to do the exam, so you can take a few minutes to get ready." I nodded. He patted my shoulder and left the room. Deflated, I dressed in the paper gown, trying in vain to keep it closed. My belly peeked out the gap in the front.

I patted it absently, thinking it would either be my belly sticking out of the front or my huge butt sticking out of the back.

I really wanted to see Dr. Al.

## The Ninth Day

### June 26, 2002

### 7:00 a.m.

"Hey, how're you feelin'?" Jeff asked, sitting on the edge of the bed, looking pleased that I was awake.

I looked around, savoring my first night's rest in a week.

I smiled weakly. For once, there was no pain.

"Good," he said. "Are you calling Dr. Al today? He's supposed to be back from vacation."

"I dunno," I said. "The pain's gone again. Plus I went the other day and it was just a bug." The Danger Voice, loud and obnoxious, argued with me and had been joined by additional insistent voices that lived inside my head. Together, they sounded like a bossy chorus.

Jeff cupped my face in his hands. "Call. The. Doctor."

"Okay." I was too weak to argue.

"I've got to get to class." He kissed me and headed for the door. "Call me if you need anything. I'll leave my phone on."

I nodded, flipping on the television, all the better to watch the clock. This time, I waited until 8:03, and asked once again for the nurse.

"This is the nurse, what can I do for you?"

I explained, again, my plight of the last week and a half, sure that I wasn't going to be allowed back in the doctor's office. I was convinced she would tell me to wait it out. Impatient with my own condition, I felt like a nuisance. Worse, I knew nobody believed me.

"Who's your doctor?" she asked.

"Dr. Al."

"Well, he's back from vacation today. Can you come in at 10:30?"

I sat speechless for a moment. "Yes," I stammered. Hanging up, I inventoried my appearance. I hadn't showered in two or three days. My matted hair hung in my greasy face. I stunk like a mixture of sleep-induced halitosis and the musty scent of clothes that have sat in a dresser drawer too long. I badly needed to get cleaned up.

*   *   *

I left a voicemail message for Jeff, not wanting to disturb him in class. I thought we'd be done around the same time; maybe he could pick me up and we could have lunch somewhere. Maybe I'd be able to eat today!

Savoring the prospect of a cheeseburger with fries, I sat in the waiting room willing the pain to stay – it had begun again during my shower. I wanted it with me during my appointment.

The nurse called my name for the next exam room and again wanted a urine sample. The cup stared at me while I worked to relax, but the thumping drum of the pain distracted my bladder. I finally produced a murky, brown sample.

I sat on the exam table, between the stirrups. The paper that covered the bed crinkled while I swung my feet over the edge of the table. I heard a faint knock at the door.

Not waiting for an answer, Dr. Al appeared, studying my chart.

"How are you?" he asked, looking into my face, his soft brown eyes narrowed. He was stout, strong and rested from vacation, back to work in his trademark scrubs.

Looking back at him, the dam broke. Tears streamed down my face. My throat closed. I couldn't catch my breath.

"I'm so sick!" I yelled. "I'm sick. I don't know what's wrong. There's this awful pain and it won't go away!" I clutched the area beneath my breasts, where the pain came and went.

Dr. Al sank onto a rolling stool. Studying my face, he handed me a box of tissues. He asked me several questions, considering ideas and then dismissing them, his face marked with concern. I waited, determined not to be sent back home to "wait it out."

Rolling over closer to me on his stool, he pressed his finger to my forearm a couple of times.

I now considered him, a bit confused.

"Well," he sighed, "you seem a little dehydrated, so I think I'll send you over to the maternity ward for some IV fluids. We may keep you for the rest of the day and possibly overnight."

My heart jumped. He believed me. I hadn't always been believed, and I didn't have the energy to fight.

He made sure I was looking at him. "The maternity ward is on the third floor of the hospital. Can you walk from here or do you need a wheelchair?"

His office building and the hospital were connected by a breezeway about 100 feet long.

"I can walk," I said, still mopping my face with tissue. "They'll be waiting for you," he said, opening the exam-room door. "And I'll see you after you're all settled in."

### 11:50 a.m.

"Kelly Wilson?" a friendly voice greeted me as the doors to the maternity ward swung open.

The owner of the voice was a curly blonde with a face as pleasant as her voice. Everything about her was soft and comfortable. Her hospital badge said "Judy" underneath her picture.

"Yes," I said with a feeble smile, my face clammy. The breezeway turned out to be longer that I'd expected, and about halfway through I wished I'd chosen the wheelchair.

"Come on over here." She directed me to the first room on the left. It was a delivery room.

She spotted me looking around. "We're delivering so many babies right now; this is the only available room. Right in there." She handed me a cloth gown and pointed to the bathroom. "It's all ready for ya."

"Ready for me?" I asked through the door.

"Yep, we need urine and a stool sample from you, so go ahead and save your samples in the cup in the toilet."

I looked down at the toilet and sure enough, instead of looking directly into the bowl, there was a large cup that attached to the rim of the toilet underneath the seat. It reminded me of an upside-down hat, but with handy points of measurement inside – metric and standard, respectively.

Stool sample, I thought. Stool sample? I hadn't eaten solid food in a week, much less produced stool. I began to coach my gastrointestinal tract into producing something that may remotely resemble stool. Come on! You can do it! I cheered my bowels on to success.

The measuring toilet hat mocked my efforts while my intestinal tract remained still and quiet. I gave up, and with the gown as secure as possible, I headed for the bed with relief. I just wanted to lie down.

"Hold on," Judy caught me at the bedside. "Gotta hook you up."

In less than a minute, my baby's heartbeat echoed through the fetal monitor attached to my belly. I watched numbers fluctuate on a machine to the left of my bed.

"OK, a couple more things," Judy adjusted the blood pressure cuff on my left arm and readied my IV.

Needles make me queasy. And sweat. I looked away. All of the other monitors were behind my head. I looked away from the fetal monitor and lay back, adjusted onto my side, relieved to be taken care of.

*   *   *

"Hey, honey, how're you feeling?" Jeff asked for the fiftieth time that week, kissing me on my cheek.

"Glad to be here," I smiled. "Now maybe I can get better."

We chatted the minutes away while Judy flitted in and out of the room. The blood pressure cuff intermittently squeezed and released my arm. The IV trickled, and the baby's heart pumped steadily.

Judy came in. "How are you doing?" she asked, studying the monitors behind me and checking my IV.

"Good," I smiled up at her. She wasn't looking at me. She was looking at Jeff.

It was a quick glance, but I caught the concern on her face right before she smiled back down at me.

"What's your usual pulse rate?" she asked.

"Heck, I've no idea," I answered after thinking on it a moment. "What is it now?"

"It's about 50."

"Is that ok?"

"It seems low."

I tried in vain to look at the monitor behind my head. At that moment, I really wanted to know my typical pulse rate.

"The doctor will be here soon," she reassured me.

"I think I've got to go," I stated. Some of my gastrointestinal cheerleading had done some good.

Jeff and Judy assisted me to the bathroom. We unhooked the blood pressure cuff, fetal monitor, and struggled to keep the IV tubes intact while I headed for the toilet. Luckily, I was able to complete my business alone.

The sample was less than impressive – a black glob due to recently ingesting charcoal pills as suggested by the nurse to relieve the stomach pain. Regardless, it was the best I could do. I congratulated my bowels on a job well-done.

Getting set up again, the blood pressure cuff immediately squeezed my arm. Judy shot another look at Jeff. Someone called her from the hallway.

"I'll be back," she reassured.

## 1:30 p.m.

Judy came in and checked my monitors, fidgeting as if she were waiting for something.

Dr. Al walked in and nodded to Judy. She stood by my head, near the IV stand.

"How are you feeling?" Dr. Al asked, sitting beside my bed, taking my hand.

"Been better."

He smiled, but it was short-lived and replaced with a serious look. I wasn't sure what that look meant.

"You're very sick," he said. "I've taken so long getting up here because I had to do some research on your condition."

I stared at him. He spoke softly as usual, but his tone harbored an intensity I hadn't heard before.

"It looks as if you have a form of preeclampsia called HELLP syndrome, spelled H-E-L-L-P. Each letter stands for a condition of this pregnancy disease. H stands for hemylosis, which is a breakdown of your red blood cells...."

I started to feel dizzy. I willed my eyes to focus on his face, my brain to understand his words. I knew they were important, but I was so tired. He spoke faster than I could comprehend.

"EL stands for elevated liver enzymes, which is what's causing you so much pain in your side. The LP stands for low platelets."

He paused, allowing me to catch up. I didn't understand what he was getting at. I felt Jeff take my other hand.

"What does this mean?" Jeff asked.

*Thank you*, I thought.

"It means we're going to have to deliver your baby," he said.

I looked up at the ceiling, calculating how far along I was in this pregnancy. Twenty-nine weeks. Twenty-nine weeks couldn't be long enough to deliver a healthy baby. Maybe we have a couple of weeks to go. I think I could do it with a couple more weeks to prepare.

"When?" I asked.

"As soon as possible. Probably tonight."

I took my hand from Jeff's grasp and clutched my head. Tears flowed immediately, dripping onto my pale green hospital gown.

"If we don't deliver, it means death for you and the baby. Delivery is the only way we know to stop this disease," Dr. Al finished.

We sat in silence for a while. I tormented myself with all I may've done to bring on this tragedy. I worked too hard, I exercised too much, I didn't eat enough vegetables, I was too stressed. I had to know what I'd done.

"What did I do wrong?" I whispered, looking at Dr. Al.

"Oh, nothing! There's no known cause for this disease," he said, patting my hand. "Don't give that another thought."

Jeff got up and began to pace. "What do we do now?"

Dr. Al sat back and switched gears. He obviously had prepared. He didn't let go of my hand.

"First we need to put you on magnesium sulfate through your IV. Your blood pressure is dangerously high, and we need to stabilize you so that you can ride in an ambulance. It'll also keep you from stroking out or going into a coma," he paused. "The drawback is that it makes you feel nauseous and overheated. Pretty soon, an ambulance will arrive to take you to Legacy Emanuel hospital. They're the best for cases like this," he answered Jeff's unvoiced question.

Dr. Al turned to me, his eyes studying my face. "Okay?"

I nodded, using the bed sheet to wipe my face.

Judy jumped into action, juggling IV bags and making the necessary adjustments. She set out some washcloths and kidney pans while I gave Jeff a list of people to call.

\*\*\*

"Is that one full?" Jeff whispered in my ear. I nodded, spitting into the kidney pan before trading him for an empty one.

I sat on the edge of the bed, hunched over. I clutched the kidney pan while I retched. My formerly clean hair hung in my face in matted ropes, splashed with my vomit. Sweat poured from my body, making the cloth gown cling.

I could feel more hot foam rise in my throat. That's all I had left to puke – scorching foam. I wanted to pour some cold water on my raw esophagus. Jeff held a chilled washcloth on the back of my neck.

Dr. Al appeared.

"How long until the ambulance?" Jeff asked.

I didn't hear the answer. I had more pressing issues on my mind.

"I'm hot! I'm so hot!" I yelled at Dr. Al between erupting mouthfuls of foam.

"It's the medication," Dr. Al stated sympathetically, and he patted my back before leaving the room.

\*\*\*

The vomiting began to let up and I leaned back, exhausted.

"The ambulance is here," Judy informed us, mopping my face with a washcloth. "I'm going to ride with you to the hospital so that your husband can drive his car there."

I nodded and looked for Jeff. He was at the sink, rinsing out kidney pans.

Two medics entered. "I'm Bob," said the older of the two. His face was gentle and experienced.

"May I take this?" he asked, gesturing at the empty kidney pan clutched in my death grip. Stomach roiling, I stared at him, daring him to take it.

Compromising, he handed me what appeared to be a plastic freezer bag with a biohazard symbol on it. I reluctantly surrendered the kidney pan. The bag was more difficult to maneuver. I'd determined that I wouldn't suffer what I considered to be a final indignity...I would not throw up on myself.

Hoisting me onto the gurney, Bob directed Jeff on driving behind the ambulance. "Follow close, but don't do anything crazy."

Jeff nodded, keys in hand.

*   *   *

Hannah and I sat in silence for a moment, a welcome pause to the intensity of the story of Aaron's birth. I breathed in slowly, the vanilla Yankee Candle scent filling my senses.

"Do you know why the scent is vanilla?" she asked.

I started, wondering for a moment if she had mad mind-reading skills. "No," I said.

"Research has shown that it calms people down. And I just like it."

I nodded, appreciating the inane quality of this conversation. "I like it, too."

"How did you feel about having kids?" asked Hannah. And there it was.

I shrugged. "Ambiguous at best."

"At worst?"

"Afraid. That I would be a terrible mother. I didn't really feel maternal, like 'warm and fuzzy'."

"And your own family wasn't the greatest."

I smiled. "That, my friend, is an understatement." Tears spilled onto my cheeks.

"I prefer you call me Jewish Mother," she said. "I served with the Israeli Defense Forces, you know."

I didn't know, but she told me about it for the next ten minutes, a welcome break in the conversation while I calmed down.

"How did you and Jeff decide to have Aaron?" Hannah asked, circling back to the issue.

"You know Jeff is ADHD, right?" Hannah nodded.

"I told him that we could have kids once the kitchen had been remodeled – the cabinets were plywood, sponge-painted white and baby blue, they were terrible – and I didn't really think he'd ever get it done. I mean, he was a busy high school band director who needed to finish his Master's degree."

Hannah pursed her lips and pushed up her glasses. "How'd that work for you?"

I chuckled. "In the space of eight months, he'd renovated the kitchen, gotten me pregnant, and watched his wife and son almost die in the hospital. It went pretty fast."

# 6

## Between Life and Death

### *The Delivery*

"DON'T FORGET THE CHICKEN," I said, gripping Jeff's arm. "I just bought a ten-pack of fresh chicken breasts, and they've got to go into the freezer before they rot," I explained. Why had I left them in the refrigerator? I'd waited too long to freeze them!

Jeff nodded, patting my hand and glancing across the bed at Linda, my nurse. She was busy setting up the same show I'd been hooked up to earlier that day in a spacious delivery room, and this time I was sure it was intentional.

She nodded. "Just get some rest," she said quietly, fitting me with a blood pressure cuff.

Rest? The pain was back, and worse than ever. Blinded by fatigue and pain, I could no longer follow people's comings and goings or conversations.

All I could think about were chicken breasts.

### *6:30 p.m.*

"We've got to do an ultrasound, and we'll be taking blood samples every few hours to keep track of her platelets," a voice explained to Jeff.

I lay as still as possible on my side, wanting to die. Sweaty, swollen, burning from the inside out, the combination was too much. I wanted it to end.

I stirred at the rumbling of the ultrasound machine being wheeled into my room. Bedside service.

I don't remember the feel of the slippery gel on my belly. I don't remember hearing the baby's heartbeat or watching his image on the ultrasound screen. All I remember is the ultrasound technician, brutally efficient, pressing unapologetically into the throbbing, stabbing, relentless pain.

I glared at her. I wanted to scream at her to not press so hard. She ignored me, working mechanically and as quickly as she could. Her movements reminded me of a robot. I pressed back into the bed, trying to escape from her. I silently cried.

I hated her.

Linda stopped at the door, surveying the progress. "Can she have something for the pain?" Jeff asked, catching Linda's eye. "After the ultrasound."

The shot stung more than it actually hurt. The rush of fluid underneath my skin surprised me, and I cried out. The heat spread out like ripples of water. It slowly abated, the heat replaced by a dull throb, and then nothing.

I hate needles.

Getting stuck with this one? Totally worth it.

## June 27, 2002 3:30 a.m.

"It's time," yelled a voice as stark fluorescent light filled the room.

Jeff, across the room on his sad excuse for a fold-out bed, sprung up into my line of vision, like a jack-in-the-box without any fun music.

"If you've got people to call, do it now," the voice told him.

I decided to lie still. Nobody had directed me to do anything, and I was tired. No luxurious sleepy morning for us, slowly waking up to breakfast and news about our delivery. The waiting was over.

I now had a sense that the atmosphere around me had intensified. Jeff got on the phone to call his parents and my mom. His tone was short, the conversations brief. People came in and out of the room, checking monitors and making adjustments. It was a stark contrast to earlier in the morning, when a nurse apologetically snuck in the darkened room to draw blood.

I waited, dozing. Time meant little to me.

Two nurses eventually came in, decked out in scrubs from their shower capped heads to their bootied feet. They were fresh-faced and alert.

"Hi, Mrs. Wilson," the nurse closest to me began, "when you have your C-section, you'll be anesthetized at the very last moment. That means we need to do your pre-op procedures...now." She paused, allowing it to sink in.

Her words meant nothing to me.

Absorbing my blank stare, she brought her tools over on a rolling tray. "We need to start with the catheter," she explained, clearly apologetic.

I stared at the ceiling and let my tears run into my ears.

I'd discovered a new final indignity.

## 5:00-ish a.m.

The gurney rolled smoothly into the operating room. I shivered and listened to idle chatter about the summer plans of the doctors awaiting my arrival. They talked about golf, and I remembered I was supposed to work the next day at the golf course. No more Beer Cart Girl job for me.

I tried to look around, but my head felt locked in place, frozen in fear, staring at the overhead lights. I'd never broken a bone, much less been in the hospital for surgery. I had visions of abruptly waking from the anesthesia – it hadn't worked properly, every nerve ending slashed by the scalpel, screaming in agony.

A face suddenly interrupted my view. It had a mint green scrub hat and a mask over its nose and mouth. Alert brown eyes looked into mine.

"I won't let them start cutting until you're out," she said kindly, quietly so that only I could hear.

## First Glimpse

While I hover between life and death in the operating room, Jeff waits alone in the hallway, unable to sit.

"There's a conference room right over there." The nurse gestures across the hall. "That may be a more comfortable place to wait."

Jeff politely refuses. He stands at the closed door and stares through the narrow window. The room he stares into connects to the operating room on its other side, where his baby, Aaron, is being born ten weeks before his due date.

The sterilized room holds basic equipment to process a new baby. He studies a scale sitting near an Isolette table with a heater attached to keep the baby warm. On the opposite side sits a stool in front of a small writing table. Counters line the walls, broken by a sink and the doorway leading into the operating room.

A crew of specialists waits in the room, sterile in every way but their faces. They talk with familiarity, the enjoyable chit-chat of people used to working together.

An EMT walks into the room, a colleague it seems they haven't seen for a while.

They greet him with handshakes and smiles; all but one who is keeping constant watch on the door that separates them from the new baby.

The EMT exits.

An OR nurse rushes the baby onto the table. All chatting stops. Smiles morph into frowns of concentration.

It's a boy. He lies limply on the Isolette table; he's about the size of a nurse's forearm. He weighs approximately two and a half pounds. The crew surrounds him, intent on helping him breathe as soon as possible.

Jeff watches as they try to insert a breathing tube into his son's throat. They try and try again. Seconds stretch into minutes.

He senses a collective sigh as they are successful. One of the crew turns on the monitor that shows Aaron's heart rate. It springs to life, registering a steady pulse. Jeff's shoulders relax slightly as he exhales. How long had he been holding his breath?

The crew slows down a bit, gradually resuming conversation as Aaron stabilizes. Jeff sees one of the crew carefully place a diaper the size of his palm loosely around Aaron's bottom. One of them sees him at the window, and walks toward him.

"You can come in and see him now," she says, giving Jeff a hopeful smile.

"How's my wife?" he asks.

"She'll be in recovery pretty soon, and then we'll know more."

## Recovery

My eyes flutter in the gray light of mid-morning. "She's awake," someone mutters.

Jeff asks me questions. I'm too tired, I want to protest, but I can't speak. My lips clamp together.

"Does anything hurt?"

I roll my head from side to side on my damp pillow.

"If it does, there's a morphine button pinned to your gown."

I look down but can't find it. He guides my hand to it. Morphine? I don't want to get addicted. Ice chips in a paper cup on the side table. I keep reaching; they get farther away, zooming out like an optical lens. Why can't I reach them?

Good friends come in; they stand far from the end of my bed.

I smile, but they look mad; why are they mad at me? Blood pressure cuff squeezes my arm.

Look, flowers and a balloon and a blue bear for Aaron. It's a Boy. Where is Aaron? Jeff shows me a picture, a profile of a baby's head with a white tube taped to his mouth. "He's so beautiful, he's doing great."

Now it hurts. Click the button, over and over, click...click...click. Feels numb again. Eyes close. Darkness.

# 7

# Under the Influence

## *Evil Wheelchair*

**THE WASHCLOTH** warmed my face, cleaning away the dried sweat from the night before, which had soaked through my gown to the sheets below me. My scalp itched with it. I smacked my lips together, loosening the layer of gunk from the surfaces of my mouth.

"Can I brush my teeth?" I asked, eyes clear, washcloth abandoned on the tray pulled from the side of my bed.

Linda stuck her head out of the bathroom door at the foot of the bed. "Sure!" she said.

She set a toothbrush and a trial-sized tube of toothpaste onto the tray. "Here are a cup to rinse with and a cup to spit," she said as she left.

I brushed, rinsed, swished, and spit. The mint of the toothpaste woke my stomach, dormant and neglected for the last week and a half.

"I'm hungry!" I stated to the empty room.

"Want some soup?" Linda asked, re-entering with more toiletries and a clean gown the mint-green shade of the toothpaste.

"Yeah," I said, handing her my teeth-brushing cups.

I reclined, looking out the picture window to my left. Sheets of warm rain pelted the Fremont Bridge, arched high above the cars traveling back and forth across it. *All of those people are living their own lives and don't know about me watching them. Where are they going?*

The empty room was silent. There hadn't been much peace, with nurses, family, and friends coming and going. Flowers and stuffed animals decorated every spare surface. I had vague recollections of visitors and of wondering why they looked upset with me. Nobody had been allowed to stay long.

"She can't take the stress," Linda had admonished many a visitor, finally hanging a "NO VISITORS" sign on my door. I'd felt bad about her escorting them from the room, over and over again.

Linda buzzed into the room and placed a Styrofoam cup of broth onto my tray with some packages of saltine crackers.

"Linda?" I asked.

"Hmm?"

"I'm really sick."

She nodded, looking me in the eye.

"If I lived in Africa, would I be alive right now?"

She narrowed her eyes. "No."

I nodded and surveyed the tray while she adjusted the pillows behind me and turned to leave. In a different time and place, I would've balked at broth, but these weren't ordinary circumstances.

I snatched the cup, no bigger than a mug of coffee, and cradled it under my chin, spooning furiously.

About halfway through the soup, Linda rolled a wheelchair into the room. I set the cup down and lay back, full and exhausted.

She rolled the wheelchair to the right side of my bed, about three feet away. It waited, staring at me, its back to the wall.

"This is for later," she said. "Get some rest." I gladly took her advice.

*  *  *

I woke to soft voices. Jeff and his parents were talking by the window.

"How was the cafeteria?" My voice croaked from lack of use.

Conversation stopped abruptly, and Jeff walked over. "Not bad," he answered. "I see that you had something to eat."

"Yeah."

"And the wheelchair?"

"That's for this afternoon," Linda said, checking my blood pressure monitor. "How do you feel?"

"Better."

"Can you move your legs and toes okay?" I nodded.

"Bathroom urges yet?" I shook my head.

"Then this is a good time to start."

"Start what?" Jeff asked.

"Well, she's got to use the bathroom eventually, so she's got to be able to sit up and get into the wheelchair."

"Then she can see Aaron," he said. "Right."

I looked at the wheelchair, sitting expectantly, arms held out to me. Just a few steps from my bed, it beckoned. How hard could that be?

"But first, you need to sit up in the bed, legs over the side, facing the wheelchair," she directed.

For the next half hour, I grunted, pulled, pushed, cried, and sweated my way into that position. My tears mixed with perspiration from every conceivable pore of my body. My face contorted, and my shoulders hunched with effort. Pain from my incision blazed in my lower abdomen; the fire began to spread.

I now understood why I hadn't as yet changed into my clean, mint-green, non-sweaty gown.

"Do you know that before a week ago, I could jog three miles a day? I could hike to the top of Mt. Tabor and back down, seven months pregnant!" I looked up at Linda, who'd become my sit-up-in-bed-if-it-takes-all-day coach.

"Doesn't matter now," she said. At that moment, I hated her.

I took a break, staring at the wheelchair I now also hated, concentrating on taking slow breaths, in and out. My legs dangled over the side of the bed.

I clenched my teeth. With Jeff on my right and Linda on my left, I stood on trembling legs and shuffled the few steps required to reach the wheelchair. They turned me around and set me gently onto the seat.

I rolled my damp head back against the wall as they cheered my accomplishment.

Mt. Tabor, I thought to myself. Unbelievable.

\* \* \*

After the excitement, Jim, Evelyn, and Jeff had left for a while to get settled and rest now that Aaron and I were out of danger.

I slept for hours with Linda guarding my door to keep people away.

For that, I decided that I no longer hated her.

Once Jeff had returned, we decided to turn on the phone so friends and family could call. My mother was the first one to take advantage of this development.

"I would visit, but they won't let me in," she said, her words clipped. "Your sister said there were no visitors allowed."

My younger sister, Mandy, and her husband had obviously tried to visit over the last day or two and had been turned away. My mother had been at our house taking care of Molly, our two-year-old black lab.

"I think you could get in to visit now," I said. *And hello, how are you? I'm-fine-thank-you-for-asking,* I wanted to add. I shifted, feeling my stomach churn and pain increase around my incision. Unfortunately, they'd removed the morphine clicker, and I could've really used it at that moment.

"Well, I would really like to see my grandson," she said. "I only got to see him for a few minutes the other day."

Even though my brain felt full of cotton, I could practically hear her nostrils flare.

I appreciated her concern for me.

The exhaustion crept up slowly, and my eyelids closed, heavy. I wanted peace, just for a moment. I let the silence take over.

"Who's that?" Jeff whispered, seated at the side of my bed.

"My mom," I mouthed.

He nodded, grabbing one of the magazines somebody had brought to my room.

"And there's some bad news," my mom continued.

My stomach dropped. With her, there was always bad news, there was always something for me to fix.

"Molly got into the garage while I was taking care of the poop in the backyard, and she got Jeff's softball glove and grabbed it and chewed it up –"

*Are you kidding me right now?*

I held the phone away from my ear, shaking my head in panic. I couldn't listen; I was going to be sick –

Jeff leaned over and grabbed the phone.

"Hey, it's me. Kelly can't talk right now. Yes, later. I'll see you then." He hung up.

"No more phone calls for a while," Jeff said, as he turned off the phone. "I'll tell Linda. You sleep."

He kissed me on the forehead. I nodded and closed my eyes.

## The Space-Age Isolette

"Are you ready to see him?" Jeff asked the next day, pushing the required wheelchair in front of him.

They'd taken it out earlier, giving me more room to swab down and change into my crisp gown. My greasy hair gathered into a ponytail, my face freshly washed, and my drugs adequately replenished, I was ready to take a ride.

Jeff helped me into the wheelchair (easier by far this time around) and pushed me through the door of my room.

Sun peeked through a wall of glass plaques lining the hallway on my right. I squinted, trying to make out what was written on them. Later I would read names of contributors and babies honored with those plaques, over and over again as I traveled the hallway.

The end of the glass hallway led to the security door of the Neonatal Intensive Care Unit (also known as the NICU), a camera mounted on its left side and a phone on its right. Jeff lifted the phone. "We're here to see our baby, Aaron Wilson," he said.

"Now, show them your wrist," he said, holding his arm up toward the video camera. Looking down at my own arm, I saw that we both had purple plastic bracelets, the latest fashion craze for the parents of premature babies.

Apparently pleased with the bracelets they could see on their video monitor, they buzzed the door open. Jeff wheeled me past the sign-in desk and a floor-to-ceiling plate-glass window that showed a waiting room in perpetual disarray.

Another door led to a small room with two stainless steel industrial-sized sinks. They reminded me of working as a teenager in fast-food restaurants, washing giant chili pots and small condiment containers. Wash, rinse, sanitize.

Three people stood in line in front of us to soap and scrub, leaving through a door directly across from the one we entered. Soon it was Jeff's turn to wash his hands and arms, using his foot to pump yellow soap from a spout mounted to the wall above the faucet. In a cabinet next to the sink, he grabbed a sponge with a rough surface on one side and plastic bristles on the other. This was clearly no-nonsense hand washing.

"You've got to scrub under your nails and all the way to your elbows, no jewelry," he said.

I nodded, head fuzzy, pretty sure I would remember none of this later.

Scrubbing completed, he wheeled me through the opposite door into a sea of curtained cubicles. Each pastel-colored curtain attached to a metal track suspended from the ceiling, encasing each area for more privacy. All that could be seen were ankles, feet, and the bottoms of equipment stands and various recliners or rocking chairs that could be rolled around the room as needed.

The cubicles were neatly partitioned into rows of two across, each identified by an animal or insect appropriately fluffed up for a baby sanctuary. We were the butterflies.

About halfway down the butterfly row, one cubicle stood open, waiting with its curtain pulled to one side. We rolled up to the Isolette.

The Isolette sat on a roll-cart about chest-high, reminding me of some kind of space paraphernalia from science fiction shows in the 1960s. Red digital numbers blazed out the temperature of the environment enveloped by the thick hood of clear plastic.

On display. So close, but unreachable. I strained to look above the bottom edge, but I couldn't see him from where I sat.

"Right on time," a nurse whispered from the cubicle on the left. "It's time for him to eat."

"All right!" Jeff whispered, pulling out the video camera. "Pictures?"

"Sure," said the nurse.

When she clicked open the hood of the Isolette, I expected to hear a "*whoosh!*" The hood stood open, like a tanning bed. On the bed itself, the nurse gently changed his diaper and I heard Aaron begin to squeak in resistance, as if taking the nurse's cue; it was a whisper of a cry, barely audible but insistent.

I craned my neck to watch while she swaddled him in a blanket as if she were making a baby burrito – bottom flap up, then the right side tucked in and the left flap brought over. I inadvertently held my hand to my chest, trying to calm the heart that felt more fear than joy.

"When you hold him," she explained, "make sure his head is back a bit and his chin is up in the air, it helps keep his airway open."

I nodded, staring at Aaron. She laid his head in the crook of my left arm. He was no bigger around than the arm that cuddled him. I wanted to clutch him closer to make sure he was there. I could barely feel his weight.

He slept the sleep of the exhausted with the face of a shriveled, wizened old man. Only the monitor assured me that he was still alive.

Beautiful? I thought. There's nothing beautiful about this.

I seethed in my drug-addled anger. How could people tell me he was beautiful? How could they lie to me like that? It was obvious to me that he wasn't supposed to be here yet, that his being here was a terrible thing. He was too small, too frail. This wasn't the way it was supposed to happen. Surely this baby wouldn't live.

"He's up to 3ccs each feeding, which is every three hours," the nurse told me, putting a tiny pink and yellow crocheted hat over his dark hair. (Measuring later, I discovered 3ccs was roughly the size of a half-dollar coin when squeezed from a dropper).

"Do you need me to –" I started.

"No, you can hold him for this," she said. She held a needle-thin clear tube and a syringe of what appeared to be formula.

"Just hold him real still." She gently opened his mouth and fed the tube down his throat into his stomach. He didn't twinge or show any sign of discomfort.

She held the syringe of formula above him so that gravity carried it to his stomach. When the tube emptied, she pulled it quickly from his mouth. The way she did it reminded me of a tape measure snapping back.

"Good, no beeping," she remarked.

I slowly filtered in the different pitches of monitors that surrounded us. Every monitor held sets of numbers that corresponded to heart rate, oxygenation rate, and blood pressure checked by wires attached to different parts of the baby's body. Any blips in the numbers or the wires would result in horrifically consistent and insistent beeps of a certain pitch. Some whined, some bleated, and some moaned while others shrieked. In an open room with only curtains for separation, beeping was constant and jarring, especially if it was your baby's beep.

"We should get him back in soon," she said. "He needs to stay warm."

I looked up at Jeff. "You hold him," he said. "Will you take our picture?" he asked the nurse.

She agreed, and he bent down next to the wheelchair. He laid one arm awkwardly around it to my shoulder and his other arm next to Aaron, embracing us both.

He smiled, I smiled through my fog of painkillers, and Aaron slept as the camera clicked.

\* \* \*

"So did your mom come in for a visit?" Hannah asked.

I nodded. "I don't know exactly when. Jeff took care of all that."

"Did she stop in to see you?"

I shook my head. "To be fair, I'm not sure that Jeff allowed her to."

"To be fair?"

"Well, yeah –" I began.

"To. Be. FAIR?" Hannah asked again.

I stared at the carpet. She was holding up a mirror so that I could see the truth, but I wasn't yet ready to state out loud what I already knew.

Hannah must've seen that and instead asked, "Why did you ask the nurse about whether you would be alive if you were in Africa?"

Relieved, I took a deep breath. "Do you remember 'We Are the World'? The people starving in Ethiopia and the song by Michael Jackson and all that?"

She nodded.

"When I was ten years old, I was watching Dan Rather on the national news," I began. "I remember lying on my stomach in front of the TV, peering at the screen over my thick glasses."

I could almost feel the yellow shag carpet under my elbows and my chin on my fists, propping me up.

"They were showing video of women and children starving over in Africa along with 'We Are the World'. And I thought to myself that with just a slight change in time and place, I could be one of those people on the news."

"Really?"

"Yeah, and that was the moment I realized that the world is a much bigger place than I'd known before, and I wondered if it was just chance that I was born in America as a white girl, or if there was more than just chance," I said, frowning.

"Like God?" she asked.

"Yeah, kind of. We didn't go to church or anything. We had books by L. Ron Hubbard and a Jehovah's Witness book but not a Bible. And then I went to Africa a couple of years before Aaron was born."

"What did you see there?" Hannah sat up a little straighter, leaning forward.

"Toilets. All kinds of toilets."

*   *   *

Even though I was an Army brat and spent a good part of my life traveling, I'm not a very good traveler. In fact, I call myself The Fussy Traveler.

When I was in high school, I went on a Missions trip with my youth group to Mexico in which we spent a couple of weeks in the desert with just an outhouse for our waste needs. When we arrived in San Diego and I was able to use an American toilet again, I flushed it and burst into tears.

Apparently, standard American toilets have always been important to me.

The sheer variety of toilets that I might encounter in Kenya didn't even occur to me as I packed for my trip. I was set to travel with a group from my church for three weeks during the summer of 1999. We split our time between light construction work and bringing a Vacation Bible School program to area hospitals, orphanages, and schools.

Part of our training for the trip included learning key words in Kiswahili. Choo is the Kiswahili word for bathroom or toilet. The word looks like the end of a sneeze, as in "ah-choo," but really, you pronounce it "cho," like the word "go."

I got my first taste of the choo at the airport in Nairobi. The stall had no door, and the toilet was missing. Rather, the toilet bowl was in the floor, with the tank mounted above my head. There was no seat on the bowl and no toilet paper anywhere in the stall. There were certainly no butt gaskets to be found, those paper protectors that end up sticking to your butt instead of the toilet seat.

I took a deep breath to steady my nerves after my twenty-four hours of air travel and instantly regretted it. The smell reminded me of the dumpster behind my apartment building at home.

But I finished my business, which took awhile, and got in the van with my group to head to our base camp in Kitale, a small city northwest of Nairobi.

The van bumped over red clay roads, and I was relieved that I had already emptied my bladder. Fascinated, I stared out the window at villages of huts made of sticks and mud with thatched roofs. Shepherds in roadside fields herded bleating sheep or goats, and women carried bundles of wood or clothes on top of their heads. Smoke from cooking fires tickled my nose and throat.

Since Kitale was a four hour drive, it was time to empty my bladder once we arrived at base camp. Our host informed us that Kitale had shut off its water supply, so instead of toilets, there was the outhouse.

"Wait, the base camp shut off the water, or the city of Kitale shut off the water supply?" I asked our host.

"It's a bit more complicated than that," he said. "The city had no money to pay the water company, so the city doesn't get water until they can pay their bill."

This explained the presence of rain barrels everywhere we looked.

The outhouse was a shack made of sticks and mud and a piece of wood lying on the ground with a hole cut out of the middle. I held the flashlight under my chin and lifted my skirt, attempting to shimmy out of my underwear enough to crouch over the hole, not drop the flashlight, swat flies out of my face, and not pee on my clothes or myself. I also tried not to cry.

I worked hard to ensure an empty bladder when leaving base camp. During our visits to schools and orphanages throughout the trip, our group gave a puppet show, which was usually "Noah's Ark" or "Daniel and the Lion's Den." My job was to perform as different characters and play with the kids who came to our shows. I learned songs, dances, and games from them, my new friends.

Our hosts from base camp walked with us, introducing me to boys and girls and telling me their stories. One boy had lost both parents to illness, while one girl farmed so that she could afford to go to school. It cost about $25 a year for a child to go to school there – about as much as it cost for a family to go to one movie at home.

There were so many of these stories. Before I went to sleep each night, I stared into the darkness and thought about the kids I had met. Soon I would go home to my friends and grocery stores and toilets that I was used to, and I felt guilty and glad at the same time.

The next afternoon, there was no way to avoid using the bathroom at the orphanage we were visiting. I made my way to a small concrete building with a wooden door and tiny windows along the top.

Inside, there was a square hole, smaller than my hand in the middle of the dull gray floor. Scrawled on the back wall above that tiny hole were the words: PLeAse Do NOT pee oN ThE CoNCreTe."

I took a deep breath. This was the most challenging choo yet. I didn't really want to stop and think about what would happen should my pee decorate the pitted concrete floor. Although the word "please" was present, the message hid a not-so-veiled threat of a mysterious kind.

I lifted my skirt and took my underwear off – I didn't need the complication of trying not to pee on my clothes. I considered getting naked from the waist down but filed it away as an option "just in case."

To keep my underwear away from the mysterious stains around my feet – it was entirely possible that these were remnants of the urine-ous kind – I wore it on my wrist like a bracelet. A thin, cotton, and somewhat tattered pair of panties that my grandmother would probably wear now decorated my arm.

I backed up, straddled over the hole, skirt gathered up underneath my chin, legs bent at the knee. I cautiously relaxed my pee muscles.

Drip, drip.

Splash. Missed the hole.

I shifted a little to the right. Dribble. Dribble.

Dang it! Missed again. The drops darkened the outside of the hole in the floor. Surely this whole situation was created by a male who had the luxury of seeing where he was aiming.

I stood still for a moment, listening for any potential consequences of my pee hitting the concrete.

Silence. No footsteps or grumbling outside my concrete choo challenge.

I shimmied a little to the left, squatting down just a little closer to the tiny hole.

BINGO.

This was, by far, the most challenging of the toilets I've encountered during my travels. But compared to the challenges faced by the kids I met, toilets were not problems.

\* \* \*

"For me, the toilets and the kids are forever united in my mind when I think of Africa, for better or worse," I said. "The suffering in the schools and orphanages, problems with HIV and health care. And I still wonder about whether there's just chance, or something more than that."

"Do you have an answer?" Hannah asked.

I smiled. "No, especially after Aaron was born."

# 8

# No Time for Denial

## *The Nipple-Distorting Vacuum*

**"WHERE ARE WE GOING?"** I asked.

"You have a new room," Jeff answered, rolling me through the double doors to the "family rooms" of the maternity ward.

We glided past a procession of light-colored wood doors, all closed, many with signs proclaiming the victory of continued pregnancy. "36 weeks and 2 days!" a banner exclaimed at me. Thirty-six weeks must be nice, I thought.

My room was on the left. Jeff returned the wheelchair while I reclined in the bed. Dozing, I startled awake as my door shut and a hard plastic package hit my leg.

"Hi!" said a chipper voice. "I'm Melissa, and it's time to pump."

Pump? I thought. My breasts had become a low priority.

She reviewed the necessary materials and instructions with me. There were two plastic cones, similar to the top of a funnel. Only at the bottom of the funnel was an inch-long cylinder wide enough to clamp to the breast and stretch the nipples so that they became unrecognizable. Below each nipple-destroying cylinder was a tube that ended in what resembled a lid – this was to screw the bottles onto, collecting breast milk.

While Melissa explained how this mysterious apparatus worked, she screwed a tiny 30cc bottle to the bottom of each cone. She then rolled a pump that had been hiding at the right side of my bed, looking innocent up to this point.

It was basically a metal box mounted on a rolling stand. The encasement was clear in order to view the pumping arm. She flipped a switch, and it began to wheeze and grind like the wheels of a steam engine train, pushing back and forth to create the necessary nipple-distorting vacuum.

I hooked up the tubes from the pump to the cones and mounted the cones awkwardly to my breasts, wishing I had a third arm. Making sure there was a tight seal between my breasts and the cones, I watched with fascination as my nipples stretched the full inch of the cylinder.

Surprisingly, I discovered that milk didn't just squirt out one giant nipple hole as I had imagined. Instead, milk spurted out of several tiny holes over the surface of the nipple. With each pulsation, the milk sprayed down through the filters into the bottles below.

*So, this is how a cow feels,* I thought.

The room grew silent as we watched the nipple distortion. After twenty milk-squirting minutes, I had collected a grand total of 25ccs of colostrum, 15ccs in one bottle and 10 in the other. Obviously, one udder was not performing up to par.

"Whoa!" Melissa congratulated me. "This is a great start!"

She walked me through the details of keeping all the pumping apparatus clean and handed me reading material about breastfeeding. She pointed out the stringent schedule required for successful milk production – I was to pump every two to three hours.

I hugged my sore, limp breasts to my body. Every two to three hours? What kind of job was this? What about sleeping? Bathing? I had yet to shower for the last three days.

She chuckled at my reaction and left the room with my breast milk, delivering it to the Neonatal Intensive Care Unit for Aaron's next several feedings.

My nipples ached and pulsated with the memory of the pump. They would never be the same.

## That's What I'm For

### June 29, 2002

*Shhhlllaaaccckk!*

I jumped at the sound of the curtain opening and frantically wiped my eyes.

"Hi," a nurse greeted me sheepishly. She was young, fresh-faced. She rolled a blood pressure cart in front of her and closed the door. "How's it going? Are you okay?"

I nodded, stifling the tears that wanted to fall from my eyes. They gathered instead into a hard knot at the base of my throat, so thick I could barely swallow.

I concentrated on breathing deeply, my coping mechanism since I was young. As an Army Brat, I moved around a lot as a kid, forever saying goodbye to people, including extended family. At the end of one visit with my grandmother, she took us to the airport and didn't shed a tear. When I asked my mother about it later as we flew toward yet another destination, she told me that crying means you're weak – the implication was clear: crying isn't allowed if you want to be considered strong.

So I don't cry in front of people.

Plus, crying is just unattractive. A friend of mine, Char, told me once about practicing her "cry face" in front of the mirror and advised me to practice my own before going public with it.

Since our conversations about it, I've become conscious of my own "cry face." My face puckers like the business end of a hot dog except for my mouth, which stretches in a grimace so wide as to accommodate said hotdog horizontally within it.

It's not pretty.

"I've got to check your pad and your bandage," the nurse said, watching my blood pressure on the monitor: still high. I sighed and felt the pinch of the staples underneath my bandage. They felt huge, industrial-sized, as if the doctors had stopped at the hardware store on the way to surgery.

I tried not to look down at the glistening metallic staples on my tired, taut skin. Catching a glimpse of myself in the mirror during a trip to the bathroom made me shudder. The bandage covering them was a shark's mouth, slightly open, and the staples were its teeth. Surrounding the bandage were bruises of different shades of purple, green and brown – while complementary on the color wheel, they were unattractive on my body.

"They should be taking these out tomorrow, along with the drain," the nurse explained as she inspected my bandage.

I nodded. The staples held the drain line spanning the length of my incision. Fluid dripped into a round, clear plastic container. Fighting the urge to squeeze it, I turned it around and around, watching the milky orange-red pus stick to the clear walls and then fall into its puddle again.

The nurse pointed to the two 30cc bottles of breast milk sitting on the counter by my bed, neither even half full. "Can I take this down to the nursery for you?"

I nodded in relief. I didn't want to go down there – that had started the last barrage of tears.

\* \* \*

Exhausted from my tentative shower, I dozed fitfully, avoiding the breast pump staring at me from next to my bed. Aaron's picture stood on a shelf above my bed, reminding me that I needed to pump.

There was a knock at the door, and Jeff poked his head around the edge of the curtain.

I smelled him before I saw him. He held a small, off-white paper bag with the logo of a burger place on its side.

"Grilled chicken," he said. "Want it?"

My bed already buzzed to a sitting position, I snatched the bag and reached for the foil-wrapped sandwich. Saliva filled my mouth.

"Wait, can I have this?" I tried to remember any food restrictions.

He chuckled and shrugged, granting me all the permission I may have needed.

The first bite included all important components of the sandwich – soft bun, squirting mayonnaise, pulpy tomato, crunchy lettuce, and moist tender chicken slab.

I chewed slowly, pushing the saltiness around my mouth, covering every square millimeter of my tongue, all the while gazing at Jeff in silent thanks.

"It's...so...good," I finally said. Tears streamed down my cheeks while I ate.

"Yeah, I figured you could use some 'real' food, but I never thought I'd see you cry over a chicken sandwich."

I would've smiled if my mouth, crammed already with more chicken, would have allowed it.

Another knock at the door briefly slowed me down. "Come in," I grunted.

Char breezed into the room, carrying a small cooler. "Looks good," she said, taking in my tear-stained face.

I nodded.

"Well, I brought more goodies," she smiled. Char had a great smile, usually outfitted with the latest shade of lipstick. She wore dark, trendy glasses, and brushed her unruly hair out of her face.

I smiled back, suddenly exhausted. My glorious sandwich, only half-eaten, tempted me; I handed it to Jeff, too tired and too full to finish. He was happy to help me out.

Char sat in one of the chairs beside my bed. "Chicken sandwich," Jeff said.

"Aaaahh, must be good," she replied. I nodded.

"Haven't eaten in a while."

"Yeah, I guess you don't eat much when you're at death's door," Char said.

Jeff and I chuckled, but I was confused. Death's door? What was she talking about?

"You wanna see Aaron?" Jeff asked.

"Sure!" Char said.

\* \* \*

Aaron lay on his stomach, his yellow skin nestled against colorful fleece. They had covered his eyes with soft, white material cut into the shape of tiny glasses. A band around his head held them into place. A fluorescent light beamed down on him.

Jeff stood at the nurse's station behind us, poring over Aaron's file and asking countless questions. I was thankful for his natural curiosity that came in so handy now. He asked questions that I couldn't even think about.

Char and I sat in the hospital rocking chairs, staring silently into the Isolette.

"I can't pray," I finally croaked quietly, suddenly unable to bear the weight of my terrible secret any longer.

She looked at me, and I avoided her gaze, trying in vain to hold myself together. It was no use - the tears faithfully came.

"Every time I try to form a prayer, my mind just shuts down," I tried to explain, wiping my eyes on my wrinkled robe.

Char wiped away her own tears. Her silence was comfort enough. She didn't twitch or look around uncomfortably, she didn't ask me what was "wrong" in a worried tone. She didn't even mention the cry face.

What I told her was the truth; what I didn't tell her was that, at the end of the blankness, I would torture myself with worry. Was God mad at me? What if I couldn't ask for help for my son? What if Aaron died? Would it be my fault?

"I just can't pray," I said.

"That's what I'm for," she said, taking my hand. "Just rest, I've got this."

Crying with relief, I sat in a nearby rocking chair, exhausted from the effort of visiting my son. I succumbed to sleep, while Char silently prayed beside me.

## *Just a Footnote*

I sat at the curb in my wheelchair as Jeff pulled up in the car. He jumped out and loaded our cart of flowers, cards, and pictures along with my duffle bag and Charlotte's cooler. It was time to go home.

Struggling and shuffling, I settled into the car, vowing I wouldn't cry. The late afternoon sun reflected off the building, the surrounding cars, and even the concrete with a dazzling intensity.

Staring straight ahead, I squinted, trying to adjust to this new world. My senses rebelled against the bright cheeriness of a summer's day. I struggled to remember the last time I'd been outdoors. I wanted to hole up in a dark room, one as cold and empty as I felt inside.

Jeff hopped into the driver's seat, turning to look at me. I nodded. He started the car.

As we drove out of the parking lot, I wanted to turn and stare at the hospital. Air conditioning blasting, I rolled the window all the way down and adjusted the side mirror instead. I directed it toward the third floor waiting room windows, right around the corner from the NICU's front door and my baby, sleeping in his Isolette, alone.

*　*　*

"Are you sure you want to go upstairs?" Jeff asked.

"Yes," I said. I could, after all, get in and out of a wheelchair. "I want to sleep in my own bed."

"OK," he said, carrying my duffle bag. I trudged up each step, one foot at a time. Right foot, left foot, wince with pain. Right foot, left foot, wince with pain. Jeff stood right behind me.

At the top of the stairs, I faced the empty nursery, door now closed. I turned the corner towards our bedroom.

The bed was made with fresh sheets and blankets. Our dressers were both cleared off (a monumental task), and the new taupe carpet we'd installed upstairs had evidence of vacuuming. I switched on the lamp. My stack of pregnancy books that had stood beside my bed for months was now gone.

"Who's this from?" I asked, pointing toward the gift bag on my bed. I opened the card. It was from Rachel, a friend of mine who'd driven down to visit from Seattle. She'd signed it, "You are my hero. I love you."

Crying again, I carefully sat at the edge of the bed and took the new pajamas out of the bag. They were a bright patterned green, quite unlike the pastel green of my hospital wear. She'd also included some lotion and soap; in the weeks to come, I used them as long as Aaron was in the hospital.

"Wow, those are nice," Jeff commented, returning from the bathroom.

"Where are the pregnancy books?" I asked, looking up from the gift bag.

"I put them away."

"Did you look in them?"

"For what? For HELLP?"

I nodded. "I want to read it." I'd read those books every night. Maybe there was something I had missed.

He looked around the room. "Why?"

"I want to read it!" I said again.

Going to the bookshelf, he recovered the bible of pregnancy, *What to Expect When You're Expecting*. He handed it to me. "There's not much," he warned.

I found what I wanted under the "Preeclampsia/PIH" heading. There was a footnote at the bottom of the page, two sentences long:

> 4. *In the HELLP syndrome form of toxemia the blood pressure doesn't always go up, but there is usually severe upper mid-abdominal pain, nausea, and possibly unexplained vomiting. Blood tests show Hemolysis, Elevated Liver enzymes, and Low Platelet count.*

"If you read more about the preeclampsia, then you'll find some of the symptoms there, too," Jeff said.

I stared, trying to figure out how this experience could only be worth a footnote.

"I don't think I would've found it if I tried," I said.

*   *   *

"Why did you want to look up HELLP syndrome?" Hannah asked. "Did you need to know more about it?"

"No," I said. "I felt like I'd been punched in the face, and I'm usually so prepared for everything. I wondered if there had been a way to prepare that I had missed somehow."

"Why are you always prepared?"

I shrugged. "Control, probably. I'm the only one who I've ever been able to really count on."

"That's what I meant by Learned Helplessness," Hannah said. "At some point, you learned that it was detrimental or at least not worth the effort to ask for help."

I nodded, staring at the blank white wall above Hannah's head.

"What are you thinking?" she asked.

"That it's weird that something I've used as a coping mechanism could have a word like 'helpless' attached to it."

"Hmm, well. Welcome to life," she said.

"Nice, Hannah. Real nice." This wasn't the first time she'd uttered that phrase to me, and it wouldn't be the last.

"What else are you always trying to prepare for?"

I shifted uncomfortably in the chair, deciding to speak without thinking. "For the other shoe to drop, whatever that might mean. And for people to leave."

She nodded. "I want you to consider for a moment what that preparation might cost you. Can you really ever prepare for grief?"

# 9

# Change in Perspective

## *Sending Flowers*

**I QUICKLY DISASSEMBLED** the Nipple Twister pumping equipment and placed it in the sink filled with soap and warm water. Less than a week into it, I was already a pro.

The actual production of breast milk was another matter altogether. I despondently capped the two tiny bottles from this dairy session, neither one full. My nipples still pulsed with the rhythm of the pump.

I placed two stickers carefully on both bottles. One of the stickers had information about "Baby Wilson," while the other sticker was one of a round baby chick. We had been upgraded from the butterfly area to the chick section, which meant he was no longer in critical condition.

I put both bottles with the others in the refrigerator, ready to be delivered to the NICU. In a few hours, we would arrive in the NICU, and place the half-empty bottles into our labeled bucket in the industrial-sized refrigerator. Then we could see our son, and a nurse would inevitably ask, "Did you bring any milk?"

Not "Hi, how are you?" or "Hey, how's it going?" For many weeks, I was simply a vehicle for human milk.

Free from my cow-like existence for at least two hours, I wandered into our office and faced the computer. I opened our email account, not certain how long ago I'd last used it. Sifting through the inbox, I was quickly overwhelmed by the messages that still needed to be answered from the last two weeks. Instead of reading it all, I clicked to a new, blank message.

Searching through my address book, I included addresses of friends and family I thought would be interested in an email about Aaron. I began to type a message – stopping, backspacing, and restarting several times.

"Whatcha doin?" Jeff asked, having heard my typing from the living room. He stood behind me, rubbing my shoulders.

"Just sending an email to people, letting them know about Aaron."

"Oh, well, who are you sending it to?"

I turned to face him, confused by his tone. "You know, people we know," I said, feeling as if I was stating the obvious.

He sighed and sat on the piano bench next to my chair. He took my hand.

"What?" I asked, suspicious, hearing my heart thumping in my ears.

"Well, you should know before you send it," he said. I stared at him, eyebrows raised.

"You know how I was calling people a lot, telling them about our situation?"

I nodded.

"Well, during a couple of the phone calls I learned that Bobbi was also in the hospital."

"Really?" I asked.

"And then I found out that her baby…died."

"Oh," I said. Deep in my brain, I sensed a switch flip – it was almost a physical sensation.

I took my hand away from his and faced the computer. I found her address on the email message, highlighted it, and deleted it. She probably didn't need to read how well Aaron was doing.

* * *

"Hold on a minute!" I called out, shuffling as fast as I could toward the front door. The bell had rung twice already.

The young man held a large bouquet of fresh flowers. The lilies caught my attention and remained my favorite: fuchsia with white and pink stripes, pistils jutting out.

I thanked him and clutched the vase to my chest, carrying them across the living room and into the kitchen. I set them down among the collection of other flowers and plants. I contemplated the display and thought about Bobbi.

No matter where I was or what I was doing, I almost always thought of her. She lingered on the edge of my consciousness.

I could not, however, think of what to do for her. I couldn't call her. What would I say? "Hey, you know how we both had our babies?"

My strongest desire was to visit her in the hospital, to help out the family with meals or cleaning, or even bring flowers.

Flowers.

I shuffled back to the computer, and within minutes I had surfed around three promising websites for sending flowers. There was only one that was appropriate for Bobbi, and that was the daisy – sunshine in the form of a flower.

I ordered the perfect vase full of daisies and then stared at the screen that waited for my message to be printed on the accompanying card.

I struggled for a message that conveyed the grief I felt for her. I went through several drafts: "I'm sorry for your loss," was too general. "This really sucks," wasn't comforting. "Guess what, I'm not pregnant anymore either," wasn't the right tone.

I finally decided on, "I wish I could be with you right now. I think about you always."

I completed my transaction, exited the screen, and prepared to pump more before my next visit.

## What is a Blessing?

"It's a balcony day?" Jeff asked, driving into the church parking lot.

"Definitely."

We were late for church anyway, but this was an intentional move on our part. I wanted to go, to test my limits, and I had pushed Jeff into taking me.

We shuffled to the front doors of the brick building. It was built in the mid-1980's, open and spacious. The sanctuary was shaped a bit like a circus tent, coming together at the top, outside where the steeple sat. On the inside, pews sat in a half circle, all facing the stage. The height of the ceiling allowed for a balcony above the pews.

We snuck up the stairs to the dim comfort of the balcony, settling into the plushy wine-colored velour of the pews.

The only way we could be seen was from the stage, but our view was quite extensive. The balcony jutted out from the back walls of the sanctuary, so the only people we couldn't see were those directly beneath us. There was a sea of heads below, some brown, gray, blond, some with comb-overs and one or two bravely bald.

Since we were late, we'd missed much of the music part of the service. I usually loved to sing, but I couldn't stand the pain of trying, physically or emotionally. We'd arrived in time for the last song, and that was enough to dissolve me into tears.

I stared at the cross, hanging high above the stage, its top almost reached the ceiling, and from the balcony, we sat almost even with it. Tears blurred my vision, and I couldn't concentrate on anything being said or sung.

I thought of my almost-death, and my baby. I thought about the people below who'd sent so many encouraging cards and gifts. I picked out the faces of people who'd kindly brought us meals three to four times a week. I thought about some of their words.

"You've been so blessed."

"God has blessed you so much with Aaron."

"What a miracle, it's just a miracle."

As I thought about these phrases, I seethed in my anger and guilt, because people said stupid things even as they meant well. They were trying to be comforting, but all I could think of was Bobbi.

I immediately applied to her anything said to me with any remote sense of God in it. Blessed, blessing, miracle, purpose, plan, all of those words.

Blessed? I didn't feel blessed either. I had a gouge in my belly, I still couldn't walk very well, my blood pressure remained off the charts, I wasn't producing any milk, and my son was currently captive in an ICU for premature babies. The only time I could see or touch him was during my one-hour, twice daily trek to the hospital, the purpose of which was really to deliver measly amounts of breast milk I'd managed to squeeze from my uncooperative breasts since my last visit.

I supposed I was blessed, though I didn't feel it. I suppose I had my life to be thankful for, since I had a tiny voice in the back of my head telling me that I'd almost died. And my baby, though virtually untouchable, was alive, and doing better every day. Maybe I was blessed.

But what I continued to turn over in my mind was, what if I hadn't lived? What if we had spent our days and weeks grieving for my son's death instead of at the hospital? Would we be blessed then?

Does God choose? If so, how does he decide?

My mind ran over the now-familiar faces of families in the NICU whose babies had been there for months, not weeks. The babies with seemingly insurmountable problems, who wouldn't be able to go home for several more weeks or months, and then not without some kind of machinery to support them. Of parents from several towns or cities away who had relocated to Portland and left jobs and friends and family members because this hospital was the only one that could handle their cases. What about them? Were they blessed?

What about Bobbi? Was she blessed?

Was God punishing all these people, but had somehow overlooked us? Where were their miracles? Where was Bobbi's miracle? Were we blessed just because things had gone our way this time? The cross blurred in my vision as my mind ran over my "blessings."

"I think it's time to go," Jeff whispered. I nodded and rose to leave.

# 10

# Death and Costco Pizza

THE SUN DANCED off Costco's roof as we drove into the mammoth parking lot. The front half, closest to the doors, was already filled with eager bargain-in-bulk shoppers.

Our lifestyle didn't often require buying in bulk, but it did require cheap, satisfying slices of pizza served fresh at the outdoor snack bar. Jeff sighed, looking in vain for a parking spot close to the entrance. Instead, he turned right, toward the outer reaches of the concrete ocean.

"Thanks for trying," I said.

Securely parked, I carefully lifted myself out of the front passenger seat in my new routine: Hand on the edge of the roof, first right leg, turn slightly, left leg, left hand on the seat behind me, and then lift, all together now!

I lumbered toward the road that separated the front of the parking lot from the back. Traffic was heavy, with SUVs, trucks, and cars of every kind circling the front lot, fighting for a prime spot. In the absence of a crosswalk, I chose a space between cars and crossed the road, my eye on the snack bar, shuffling one foot and then the other, favoring the healing wound on my lower abdomen.

Jeff stayed at my left elbow, his hand shadowing my arm.

"It wouldn't be so bad if I was carrying a carseat," I said. "Then people would at least know why I was taking so long."

I immediately thought of Bobbi, how she must be slowly lifting herself from cars and shuffling through parking lots and stores. She wouldn't have a baby seat to carry, not for this baby.

"What?" I said, realizing Jeff had said something I hadn't been able to hear.

"What kind of slice do you want?" he asked again.

"Cheese," I said. Jeff settled me at the picnic-style resin table and stood in line for our food.

I looked at the surface of the white plastic, reflecting the sunshine and blue sky typical of a summer's day. I tried to shut Bobbi out of my mind, tried to shut out the guilt.

Jeff returned with our food, and I ate slowly, picking the pizza apart and avoiding conversation and his eyes. Silence settled like a blanket.

"I just don't get it!" I finally exploded, ignoring my pizza.

Jeff looked at me, mouth chewing, waiting for an explanation.

"Why? Why this baby? I can't get it out of my head."

"Aaron?" he asked.

"Kind of, but Bobbi, too. I can't stop thinking about Bobbi," I finally admitted, beginning to cry.

"And then, what's worse, what's more confusing, is that my baby is alive and hers is...is dead," I whispered.

He moved his eyes to the table, no longer eating.

"And it just as easily could be me. It could be my baby who's dead."

Pizza half-eaten, both of us looked around in the heavy silence, mocked by the vibrant colors just outside the snack bar. It was already time to head to the hospital.

*   *   *

The Budweiser billboard faithfully taunted me for the second time in the same day, just as it had yesterday, just as it would tomorrow.

Buxom blonde twins flaunted cleavage, pouting sultry painted lips. The word "twins" was written in bold, red letters across their thighs, and underneath that was the beer logo. I remained mystified; apparently there was a connection between these twins and beer.

One constant on our route to and from the hospital, the billboard stayed the same for five out of the six weeks we visited the NICU. I had plenty of time to contemplate its meaning.

Twins, I thought once again, unable to tear my eyes away. I slumped in my seat, dreading tonight's visit.

"I've been thinking about something," I said. "Yeah?" Jeff asked.

"Well, in the hospital, remember when you brought me the chicken sandwich?"

"Yeah."

"Then Char came, and she made some comment about me being at death's door."

"Okaaaaay." Jeff bit his lip and squinted his eyes. Clearly he didn't remember.

"Well, I've been wondering what that was all about, that talk about being at death's door. Did I almost die?"

"Oh, yeah," Jeff answered. He seemed surprised by my question, assuming this was common knowledge. It was, just not for me.

"Really?" I turned toward him, not wanting to believe him. The idea was ridiculous.

He navigated through downtown toward the hospital. "It really didn't look good for awhile. You even had trouble after Aaron was born; your kidneys weren't working. You were really sick, Kel."

"Hmm." I looked at him thoughtfully, taking it in. "And Aaron?"

"We didn't know about him either. That's why it was so great when he was off the ventilator so quickly."

My head ached, as if realizing this information had caused my brain to swell. I hadn't thought about death before, especially not my own.

"Well, that's just weird," I said.

"What?"

"I thought there'd be some kind of moment where you instinctively knew you were going to die, and then your life "flashed before your eyes" – I inserted the quotation marks with my fingers – "and you could make your peace and say your goodbyes."

"Hmm."

Apparently that didn't happen with me, I thought. All the stuff I'd heard before, about the tunnel of light and angels or dead family members greeting people to take them to the "other side" didn't happen to me. I'd had no visions of the golden streets or crystal seas or fragrant flowering meadows stretching before me, beckoning me onward.

I had no idea. Just pain and then darkness. No significant moment, no nudge from above to "make my peace," no Angel of Death, especially not one with a black robe and scythe.

"How could you almost die and not know it?" I asked. Frustrated, I waved my hands at Jeff. "I mean, almost dead! No idea!"

He shrugged, pulling into a parking space. He seemed finished talking about my possible death. Can't say that I blamed him.

"I will not miss this place," I said, like I said every day. First anger, immediately followed by guilt and the thought, at least you have your baby.

## Would You Want to Know?

Jeff's parents, Jim and Evelyn, had returned home after it had been determined that Aaron and I would, in fact, live. They came back to visit when Aaron was about three weeks old, after Jeff and I had some time to adjust to the demands of traveling back and forth to the hospital every day.

The four of us sat in a semicircle around the Isolette in mismatched rocking chairs. I'd already delivered and pumped measly amounts of milk, surrendering my touch time so that Jim and Evelyn could have turns.

Jim cradled Aaron, who no longer resembled a two-pound Baby Loaf of Tillamook cheddar with the wizened face of an old man. He was starting to resemble what stereotypical babies look like, only minus the fat – he was a very lean baby, like Victoria's-Secret-model-thin. Jim held him as if one false move would shatter his little body.

Once his precious ten minutes were up, he handed Aaron to Evelyn. She and Jeff promptly stared into Aaron's face with rapt love and attention.

"Wow, he gets surprisingly heavy," Jim whispered to me.

I nodded as we rocked in our chairs, watching Jeff and Evelyn coo and murmur to Aaron. "It's the stress of holding him, afraid you'll break him," I answered.

He nodded. "So how are you doing, Little Girl?" Jim was the only one who was ever allowed to call me Little Girl or Baby Girl without getting punched in the face. He started using the nicknames interchangeably once I moved into Jim and Evelyn's house during my senior year of high school.

I shrugged. "I found out I almost died."

"Oh, did you?" he asked, chuckling. "Surprised?"

"I just didn't even know," I said. "I thought that if you were going to die, then you would somehow be given time or space to say goodbye to people. For me, there was nothing like that – I went to sleep and woke up a couple of days later. There were no angels, no white light, no scenes of life flashing before my eyes."

He nodded thoughtfully. If anyone would know what I was talking about, it would be Jim. He'd experienced a variety of health issues, including his first heart attack when he was only thirty-eight. Granted, a lifetime of sandwiches made of bologna slathered with Miracle Whip on slabs of Wonder bread and washed down with Pepsi didn't help.

Since that first heart attack, there'd been two or three more, along with a stroke scare and an aneurysm. To say he was "living on borrowed time" was a bit of an understatement.

"Well, think of this," he said. "Would you rather go suddenly, or would you rather know that you were dying?"

"Being the anal-retentive person that I am, I'd probably want to know," I said. "There's just so much to get done when it comes to dying."

He laughed. "So much to do, huh?" I had to laugh, too.

"Not me," he said. "I think, go quick and clean."

Neither one of us realized how prophetic his words were at the time.

*   *   *

If I'd known at the time that Costco sold caskets, I might have shared this information with Jim at this point, and we would've gotten a good laugh.

"Was it difficult to bring this up with Jim?" Hannah asked. "The almost dying?"

"No," I said. "I figured that if anyone could understand, it would be him. He'd volunteered with hospice for awhile."

"Really? Wow," Hannah said.

"Yeah, I appreciated his humor about death. In the months before he died, Jim would joke that the only plant he was comfortable growing was bamboo."

"Why?"

"So he could see it reach its full potential." I giggled. "Then he would just laugh...but all of that to say, I appreciated being able to talk with him about it."

# 11

# Floating Questions

## *Two Babies*

## *Spring 2003*

BOBBI CARRIED HER creativity and love for change on her head – her hair had always been an array of color, a creative cut, a trendy style. Curly. Straight. Flipped. Highlighted. Solid brown, or black, or blonde. Long. Short. Sometimes when looking through my photo albums, I can tell what year a picture was taken because of Bobbi's hairstyle.

Her hair has been straight and her natural color, honey brown, for the last two years, arranged simply: parted down the middle, shoulder-length, a slight flip on the ends, no bangs. A style reflecting how streamlined her life has become. She no longer has the luxury of fussing over her hair.

The Christmas after her mom died, Bobbi unexpectedly became pregnant. She was immediately excited by the thought of a new life, a symbol for the future. A new boy or girl to carry on her legacy and the legacy of her parents. Hope.

The day after I gave birth to Aaron, she gave birth to her baby girl, whom she named Hope. The doctors had no explanation for the baby's death.

Six months later, Bobbi again became pregnant. She was excited but cautious. Because of her history, her pregnancy was considered high-risk. The fact that she was having twins complicated matters a little, but she was receiving excellent care.

We celebrated each milestone – when the twelfth week came and went, the first ultrasound, and giving the twin boys their names (Billy and Carter). Bobbi was at the doctor's office constantly, and she was able to have an ultrasound at least every two weeks. The babies were healthy, she was feeling good, and the situation looked promising. She began to make plans for the eventual delivery of her twins, under her doctor's guidance, who advised her that they would probably come sooner than later.

Early in her pregnancy with the twins, Bobbi came over for a visit. With life being as crazy as it had been during the first several months of Aaron's life, it was really no surprise that this would be the first time Bobbi would see him.

An hour before she was scheduled to arrive, I stared at myself in the bathroom mirror. It was one of those rare days in a young mom's life where I was able to squeeze in a shower before 10 a.m.

I dried off and dressed as if in a dream, then brushed out my wet hair, thoughts spinning.

Was it a good idea for Bobbi to visit? What would her reaction be?

Would she simply look at Aaron and then have to leave?

Would we both burst into tears and spend the whole visit with our cry faces?

I thought I might have to take a second shower, because the sweat of the desperately anxious had popped out all over my body, and I felt like I was going to throw up. No matter what happened, I had to hand it to her. She had some pretty big *cajones* to come for a visit considering all that it might dredge up.

When she arrived, though, Bobbi simply cooed over Aaron, played with him and took pictures and generally thought, as I did, that he was the most precious and awesome kid in the world.

We didn't even have cry faces, except for one close call.

"So being pregnant with twins, when do you think you'll have to go on bed rest?" I asked.

She paused for a minute to pick Aaron up and hold him on her lap. She sighed. "Well, the doctors and I are thinking early or mid-June, and I'm going to need to quit my job because there will be two babies instead of one," she said, and then hesitated. "Since in my mind all babies die, I don't really think I'll need to quit my job."

I nodded in understanding. A small, sad smile passed between us.

Our eyes filled with tears and maybe a tear or two fell, but then Aaron did something cute, and I was able to spare Bobbi my full-on cry face.

*   *   *

At eighteen weeks, an ultrasound revealed that she had a disease of the placenta called Twin to Twin Transfusion Syndrome. This disease involves connected blood vessels within a shared placenta. Billy was receiving too much blood, overwhelming his cardiovascular system. His heart had to work too hard to pump, which could cause eventual heart failure. Carter was receiving too little blood, threatening death from severe anemia.

When the doctors confirmed her condition, they assured her that she could've done nothing to prevent it. Considering Bobbi's experience with Hope, the doctors said that it was the equivalent of being struck twice by lightning in the same place.

Because of her extensive base of support, Bobbi kept all of us informed through frequent emails. In one of them, she explained her prognosis:

*"We met with a perinatologist near Seattle today and they found that little Carter has brain damage due to not getting enough blood and oxygen for so long, and the doctor said if we don't do anything, both boys will die. He recommended the laser surgery which will disconnect the shared vessels in the placenta so the boys will grow independent from one another for the remainder of the pregnancy.*

*Although Billy looked healthy, the doctor did say that we have a 60% chance of saving him, and less for Carter because he's already so behind...."*

I forwarded these emails to friends of mine, asking for prayer and support for Bobbi. I often received replies, many of them understandably disturbed. All showed concern for my friend, and I noticed that they tended to follow a pattern. After their words of concern, there was almost always a comment like these:

"Why her?"

"It's amazing that one person has had to suffer this much pain."

"How much more can she be expected to take?"

"Why is one person allowed to endure this much suffering?"

I could only bite my bottom lip and nod slowly in agreement as I read. I breathed in, filling my lungs with air and holding it for a moment, letting it escape in frustration.

I didn't know why.

## Carter's Funeral
### Summer 2003

A refreshing breeze moved puffy clouds through a cornflower blue sky. It was the perfect afternoon for a walk in the park or lounging on a patio – perfect for anything but a funeral for a baby. Bobbi's baby.

His name was Carter, one of the twins she carried when they developed Twin to Twin Transfusion Syndrome. Billy had been safely delivered and was currently in the Neonatal Intensive Care Unit close by.

Flowers covered the headstone. Behind the headstone was a barely discernible rectangle cut into the grass, about two feet long by one foot wide.

In front of the headstone stood two chairs, covered alternately with darkness and sunlight as evergreens swayed overhead.

I'd thought about not coming at all, worried that my presence would be too upsetting to Bobbi; a reminder of how we were opposites once again.

But she'd called me, had said it was all right, that somehow my near tragedy made our friendship possible, that she couldn't really explain it.

People trickled to the graveside. Most of us looked uncomfortable; we were old friends. Was it appropriate to chat? Should we smile at each other? I found myself staring at the headstone, trying not to make jokes to myself as I coped with my own unwillingness to feel sad.

The pastor conducting the service directed us to form a wide circle around the graveside, and he placed himself opposite the two chairs now holding Bobbi and her husband, Mitchell. The pastor held a thin Bible and wore a tie with a black background and electric blue swirls. I stared, mesmerized, at the tie; it was not an electric blue kind of day.

He stood with quiet authority, faced with the difficult task of addressing a group of mourners who not only wanted comfort but also answers. Why Bobbi and Mitchell? Why Carter, and why Hope?

He preached a short sermon with an apologetic smile and blue eyes that met each person's in turn. He talked about our various births in life – conception, physical birth, relationships with others, spiritual birth, and then birth into eternal life – the idea that death isn't an ending, but a beginning, and that Hope had skipped a few steps, being born into eternal life instead of the physical one.

An attendee handed out balloons and markers for us to write our thoughts to Carter and then release into that beautiful expanse of blue. I had no thoughts.

"Ugh, this is just not good for the environment," said another attendee.

I have to admit, this hadn't occurred to me. Also, I didn't care.

My brain felt frozen. I'd expected some validation for both Carter's and Hope's death, for how terrible this was, about how death is a crazy thing that happens to us all. I didn't want spouting about birth phases and eternal life. I wanted assurance that Bobbi and I weren't the only ones who felt this terrific pain.

I turned the pink balloon over in my hands, squeaking the rubber beneath my fingertips, smelling the essence of childhood birthday parties. I wrote the only words that made sense: "We will remember you."

We will remember what it was like to lose you, our pain the black background of our electric blue joy. We will remember that there are few answers to our questions; the questions that seem to float into an endless expanse of sky.

# 12

# A Crystal Ball

*July 2004*

OUR DECISION TO HAVE Aaron was based partly on a kitchen remodel. Jeff asked me what it would take to have a baby, and that was my answer.

Almost the moment he was done with that construction project, I got pregnant. Seven months later, we had Aaron.

To put it another way, it literally took less time to remodel the kitchen and have a baby than the length of a typical pregnancy (we had a really small kitchen).

After our experience with Aaron, deciding to birth a second child wasn't such a simple, oblivious decision. First, Jeff and I had the conversation once Aaron turned a year old – for an entire year. Then, I asked Dr. Al about it at one of my routine appointments to check my Lady Parts.

Dr. Al, who was known for his cerebral brilliance, tended toward the rational. "There's basically a 12% to 50% chance of a recurrence of HELLP Syndrome or Preeclampsia," he said during our discussion. "And a 50% chance of anything at all going wrong. But it will be fine!"

When I told Bobbi about this conversation, her response was, "I think having a healthy pregnancy and birth experience is the statistical anomaly anyway. Either way, you have to take the risk."

I nodded, feeling nauseated and also at peace. Considering our situations with pregnancies and birth, the idea of a "normal" experience was an idea from the past.

Still, Jeff and I went back and forth, having the "should we have another baby?" conversation in spare moments, like while walking through the mall. We pushed Aaron in his stroller toward the play area one weekend afternoon, which had become our home-away-from home during rainy spring days with a busy toddler.

Seated on the vinyl bench that surrounded the giant foam and plastic toys that were in fact germ factories, we watched as Aaron explored. Climbing and crawling, he propelled his pudgy toddler body through the obstacles on short legs from here to there and back again.

After telling Jeff what Dr. Al had said, I asked, "So what do you think?"

"I don't know, Kel. I mean, that's a pretty wide range, 12% to 50%."

"Or just the 50% chance of anything going wrong," I answered. "But isn't that the case no matter what? There are risks with all pregnancies."

Jeff nodded. We sat in silence for awhile, smiling at Aaron as he jumped off the short plastic slide and nailed the landing.

"Basically," I finally said, "we want to know the outcome. We don't have a crystal ball. I'm not a nomad woman wrapped in scarves that travels with a carnival and tells people's fortunes with a brown mole on my upper lip that has one dark, coarse hair coming out of it."

"That's amazingly specific," Jeff said. He chuckled and sat back against the foam bench, putting his arm around my shoulders. "You need a rat to gnaw that mole off."

Once our giggling subsided, I continued. "We have choices. We either take the risks, or we decide not to. That's it."

"Okay, but what do we choose?"

"Considering what I just said —" I began.

"You want to tell people's fortunes? You have a scary mole?"

"No!" I laughed. "The risks, combined with how much I want another child, I think we should try," I said.

By the Harvest Moon of October, I was pregnant.

*     *     *

"Why did you want another child?" Hannah asked. She sat, curled up on end of her couch.

I shifted on the black leather chair across from her, lying back against one of the chair's arms and dangling my legs over the other. I pulled the brown fleece blanket up under my chin.

"Total honesty?" I asked.

"Always." Hannah grinned.

"I kind of felt like I was already in hell, so might as well get it done." I sighed. "That sounds harsh, but Aaron's birth and first couple of years kicked my ass. I knew Jeff wanted another child, and I didn't want the issue hanging out there so that in ten years I'd have to do the baby stage again."

She nodded. "That's refreshingly honest."

"I guess."

"What did you think would happen with Noah when you got pregnant?"

"I didn't think it was going to be all butterflies and rainbows," I said. "For awhile it was fine, but for me, the other shoe eventually drops. Always."

# 13

## Skip Denial, Move On to Anger

*Week 28 – I Told You So*
*April 2005*

PREGNANCY, LIKE A CAR, runs on its own odometer. Usually measured in months, pregnancy can be measured in weeks and even days. For example, Aaron was born at twenty-nine weeks and five days. I'm sure you could narrow it down to how many hours a woman has been pregnant, and maybe somebody has. I didn't have time to figure that out during my second pregnancy, as I was trying to chase two-year-old Aaron around and not pee my pants all the time.

When I arrived for my first prenatal appointment with Dr. Al for the current pregnancy, the first question I asked was when he was planning his vacation for the coming year.

We chuckled, but I was only half joking. I was at exactly twenty-eight weeks pregnant with Aaron when I first puked, signaling the beginning of that little nightmare. And like I was suspicious about "watched breasts don't produce milk," I was concerned about that 28th week.

"It'll be fine," Dr. Al assured me while checking the baby's heartbeat. "Call any time, we'll see you. Doesn't matter for what, just call."

I had to admit, that made me feel better, but I didn't actually ever have to call.

Except on the day my pregnancy odometer turned over to twenty-eight weeks.

And Dr. Al was on vacation.

\*   \*   \*

There's a little-realized fact about a woman's body: the uterus sits right on top of the bladder. I don't presume to give God a critique of His work, but surely this must be a design flaw, or at least an oversight.

Because as a baby grows inside a uterus, the pressure on the bladder is consistent and painful. By the time my pregnancy odometer reached twenty-eight weeks, I was peeing easily twenty times a day. If I sneezed, coughed, or laughed too hard, I'd have to change my clothes. I did a lot of laundry during my second pregnancy.

It was during one of these toilet trysts that I found what you never want to find when you're pregnant, and that is blood.

"I'm freaking out, I'm bleeding," I said, on the phone with Dr. Al's receptionist. My hands and my voice trembled.

"Okay, what's your name?" she asked.

Taking a deep breath, I paused and gave her my basic information, and she transferred me to a nurse.

"How much are you bleeding?" the nurse began. "Well, I saw blood when I went to the bathroom, but it seems to have stopped," I said.

"Are you experiencing any pain?"

"No."

"How soon can you get here?"

"Twenty minutes."

"We'll be expecting you."

\*   \*   \*

Time passes differently in a hospital. All can seem gradual – come in for a non-stress test. Stay for a couple of hours, and a few more hours, then overnight, and then a week. After that, we'll just see.

At my appointment, everything seemed fine, but the doctor on-call wanted to do a non-stress test to see how the baby was doing. Basically, I would be strapped to a fetal monitor while lying in a bed – not a bad way to spend an afternoon.

"How long will that take?" I asked when I arrived.

"A couple of hours," a nurse told me.

This turned out to be a gross misrepresentation of how long I'd be there. Hospital time tends to run approximately three to four times slower than regular time, and there's no controlling it.

After the nurse hooked me up to the fetal monitor, I was essentially trapped there for a couple of hours until my bladder tortured me. I thought I might be done when they let me go pee in a toilet hat, but it was a couple more hours. Then a couple more. Then overnight.

The next day, I was able to go home on the condition that I come back once per day to be hooked up to the fetal monitor for non-stress tests, and I had to take it easy. *No problem, I'll just tell my two-year old that I need to relax.*

Dr. Al was back from vacation in time for the next non-stress test, and he didn't keep me for an hour or two longer than I expected – Dr. Al kept me for a week.

By that point, Jeff and I had named the baby Noah, which would turn out to be an incredible twist of irony. I had to stay in the hospital for a week because my placenta had sprung a leak, and the baby named after the Bible character blessed with an abundance of water actually had none in which to float because all of the fluid had simply disappeared.

"The lack of fluid leads to umbilical cord compression when Noah moves around," Dr. Al explained. "There's very little fluid to keep him buoyant. If he sits on his cord for long enough, his oxygen is cut off, which can lead to stillbirth."

"I told you not to go on vacation," I said.

He smiled, patient with me as usual. "The range of fluid can be anywhere from 5 cm to 35 cm – anything below 5 cm is considered critical and the baby's delivered."

"How much do I have?"

"Between 1.5 cm and 8 cm at any given time," Dr. Al said. "So we're keeping you here for a week to pump you full of fluids, and you'll be lying down on bed rest to try and repair the leak. Hopefully all of this will help Noah stabilize."

I nodded, numb, and unable to think.

The nurse came in and prepped me for the IV that was never further than three feet away for the next seven days.

## Week 29 – So, What are the Chances?
## May 2005

"Any Improvement? At all?" I asked.

Dr. Al studied the ultrasound screen while sliding the probe around my belly.

Jeff stood on my left, peering across at the ultrasound screen as well. Aside from Noah moving around, it looked like static.

"Well, it looks like the fluid level has increased about a centimeter or two," Dr. Al said.

I stared at the ceiling, tears filling my eyes. "That's it?" The words came out as a croak, suffocated by my frustration. After bags and bags of saline pumped into my veins, along with bottles of water poured down my gullet – one or two centimeters? So his theory of trying to replace the amniotic fluid did not, in fact, hold water.

Jeff squeezed my hand. "What does this mean?" he asked.

That was the first time either one of us had asked a question like this. We'd discovered during the drama with Aaron's birth that in the hospital, words aren't as important as silence. If people aren't talking, our situation may be really bad. If we ask questions, then they'll answer them and we'll know the truth, when denial can be a lot more comfortable.

But now we wanted to know. Now we were willing to ask.

"What are the chances?" I whispered.

Dr. Al looked at us. "You really want to know?"

We nodded.

"Imagine you're driving 70 mph on a mountain road with a cliff on one side and a sheer mountainside on the other," he said. "You round the bend and see a semi-truck coming at you, taking up both sides of the road. You've got some choices – drive off the cliff, which is certain death. Drive into the semi, which is a large moving vehicle, so that doesn't look good. Or drive into the mountain wall for a better chance of survival."

I glanced at Jeff. He squeezed my hand.

Dr. Al continued, "So basically what we do each day is weigh the lesser of two evils – the chance of losing the baby from cord compression or losing the baby from premature birth, of which we are all well aware. So we'll see."

So now we knew. This was serious.

Which, in my boredom and complaining and denial, I tended to forget how serious.

I no longer had the luxury of forgetting.

## Get Out of My Bathtub...Literally

After a week of intense hydrotherapy, my condition was slightly better. Dr. Al decided that I could go on complete bed rest at home, as long as I came in once or twice a day for non-stress tests and ultrasounds.

This break only lasted three days. Was bed rest at home better than in the hospital?

Hands down. At home, I could be alone.

There's no privacy in a hospital. One nurse wanted to come into the bathroom with me because I refused to wear the fetal monitor during my shower. This led to a little paranoia on my part. Did she have a crush on me? Did she want to see my extra 25 pounds of cellulite spread evenly over my body, along with stretch marks on my hips?

Somehow she wanted to be present every minute that the fetal monitor wasn't hooked to me – I couldn't imagine what she could possibly do to help as I soaped up my giant pregnancy ass.

I wanted to scream at her, "Get OUT OF MY BATHTUB!"

At times, it took me an hour and a half to eat a meal because of the constant interruptions – nurses taking vital signs, wheelchairs arriving for ultrasound appointments, general annoying conversation.

The aggravating comments tended to cycle. For example:

"Have you thought of a name yet? He needs fluid, so maybe Noah..."

"The baby looks good. Great vitals! He's doing great!"

"That baby better behave for me tonight (or today)."

"Did you know we have a movie cart? You can check out movies."

"Going stir-crazy yet?"

The only routine was that there wasn't any routine. Nurses changed shifts every twelve hours, and as impossible as it seemed, there remained nurses that I hadn't met.

I had a white board with my stats that I changed each day – kind of like scratching a mark on a prison wall for each day that passed. The white board had the number of days I'd been in the hospital, along with Noah's gestation in weeks and days to keep track of our progress – every day counted.

One morning, a nurse disagreed with my gestation weeks and days on the board, and erased them.

It turned out that my numbers were correct (I mean, really, who should KNOW at that point?). But she still had erased them.

Unbelievable. I was P-I-S-S-E-D. Essentially powerless, but pissed nonetheless.

## Nice, But Schizoid

The only consistency for Noah's condition was that it was totally inconsistent. There would be hours – sometimes a whole day – in between episodes. I could be lying in the hospital bed talking on the phone or reading a book to the background noise of Noah's heartbeat – bump-bump, bump-bump, bump-bump – at around 130 beats per minute, when it would gradually slow down.

As his heart rate approached about 60 beats per minute – bum - BUMP, bum - BUMP, bum-BUMP – the door to my hospital room crashed open to let in a flood of nurses. Working together, they placed an oxygen mask over my nose and mouth, gently rolling me around on the bed to try to get Noah to change position. Nobody breathed as we listened, and I silently chanted, "move, move, move."

Lasting anywhere from six to ten minutes, these "cord episodes" indicated whether or not they needed to perform an emergency C-section. If Noah's heartbeat didn't come back up, or if he had enough "cord episodes" in a row, then Dr. Al would have to deliver him.

\* \* \*

The undercurrent of stress reminded me of when I visited Aaron during his first weeks in the Neonatal Intensive Care Unit, convinced that a baby the size of a two-pound block of Tillamook cheese with the face of an old man couldn't survive.

Concerned that Noah wouldn't make it, I was certain that we'd go through all this to discover some debilitating kidney disease from the low fluid, or they wouldn't deliver him in time, or there would be unforeseen complications for which we couldn't possibly prepare.

I was supposed to be moved to Oregon Health Sciences University Hospital the week before, since it's a Tier III hospital and better prepared to deal with Noah's situation. Unfortunately, nobody would accept the liability to move me (even by ambulance), so I was to stay put to deliver whenever Noah should come, for better or worse.

Dr. Al visited or called each day, and on a couple of his visits, explained to me again why I couldn't be moved to OHSU.

"Doc, no offense, but what's your point?" I asked as he sat beside my bed during his latest visit.

"Don't you want to move to OHSU?" he asked.

"No," I said. "I'm close to my family and friends. I have a room to myself, a TV, VCR, fridge, microwave, and internet access. I do NOT need to mess that up."

"Haven't you been complaining to the nurses about moving?"

"No," I said.

"You haven't been crying, begging them to call me to change my mind?" Dr. Al asked.

"What? No," I said. "What's the deal?"

"Well, the nurses have been calling and telling me that you're very upset about not being able to move to OHSU, that you're having fits and yelling."

My mouth hung open. "No. Way."

"Yeah," he said. "Although it's only the day shift." This made sense, since the night shift nurses included me in their Red Robin runs in the middle of the night – I found deep fried cheese sticks and milkshakes quite comforting.

"Unbelievable," I said. I had to respect their strategy. So the nurse on the dayshift who wanted to be in the shower with me did not, in fact, have a crush on me.

He nodded, and we both started laughing. "Not true," I said through my giggles.

Dr. Al looked fascinated. "They're nice people, but they're schizoid," he said.

I guess I couldn't blame the nurses for wanting me moved – I was accustomed to the heightened stress, but I saw women come in every day who were in labor, pushed, had their babies, stayed a day or two, and then went home in wheelchairs, holding tiny bodies and looking scared out of their minds. Seemed easy to me.

But mine was not easy.

*   *   *

"So it's clear that the dayshift nurses didn't necessarily like you," Hannah said with a smile.

I grinned. "Well, they didn't like the situation, for sure. And I wasn't an easy person to deal with all of the time, although I did try," I said, running a hand through my hair and yawning.

"What do you mean?"

"I would wake up and say to myself, 'This is going to be a good day, a better day,' and then I would be in tears by noon. But I figured out how to schedule visitors around mealtimes so that I could avoid eating the cottage cheese loaf that was always on the menu."

"Cottage cheese loaf?" Hannah asked. Her expression was a mixture of disgust and wonderment. "A loaf of cottage cheese? How? Why?"

I shrugged. "Fortunately I never had to find out because visitors always brought me food. I was at Portland Adventist, and they're vegetarian."

"Where were you when you had Aaron?"

"Emmanuel Hospital, downtown. They had pretty good food there."

"What about visitors?" she asked.

I smiled, picking up what she was throwing – well, tossing – down. "You mean, did my mom visit while I was in the hospital with Noah being tortured with something called cottage cheese loaf?"

Hannah nodded.

I leaned back in my chair, crossing my arms over my chest. "I think when Noah was born and I'd been there a month," I said. "Jim visited, though."

"Interesting."

"Yeah, he sent me an email that became my favorite while I was stuck in the hospital."

"Why was it your favorite?" she asked.

I sighed. "Finally there was a parent doing what parents are supposed to do. Instead of yelling at me or hurting me, here was a dad who was telling me that everything was going to be okay. That, no matter what, it was going to be okay because we were a family. I hadn't had that before."

## *My Favorite Bedrest Email*

*From: Jim*

*To: Jeff and Kelly*

*Subject: Re: latest news on Kelly*

*Dear Kelly, thank you for the update. I know it's difficult for everyone around your house right now, but I believe that all will end well.*

*I remember very vividly the first time I saw Aaron, in the hospital. Somehow I knew, I mean really knew, he was going to be just fine. That tiny little boy with tubes in him everywhere, so little and frail looking but I knew he was going to be okay. Kelly, I have that same feeling about Noah. It's not intuition or just wishful thinking, it's a heart thing. He is a Wilson after all!! hahaha*

*I have all of you in my prayers each day and night. In the past two years I have come to realize just how important family is. Of course I knew that on the intellectual level but on the heart level I was missing something. I treasure my family, all my family.*

*So you just hang in there, Little Girl. You and Noah are going to be just fine. That doesn't mean there won't be some anxious moments, because there will be. There will be some fear mixed in with everything else. I am not a prophet, just a man who loves his family and I know everything will turn out well.*

*Enjoy the bed rest, after Noah gets here you may treasure some of these lay-around days.*

*Love You,*

*Dad*

# 14

## Supportive, Like a Bra

### *If This Doesn't Break You*

**BY THE TIME twenty-one DAYS** had passed, I was a wreck.

I started each morning determined that this day would be better. By noon, I had dissolved in tears at least once. The rest of the day was spent moving from the bed to the rocking chair either crying, trying not to cry, or preparing to cry.

When Dr. Al was out (I guess he had to sleep sometime), other doctors at the hospital came by to check on me. One of them was Dr. Blake.

Dr. Blake was lifeguard-handsome, right out of a soap opera. I thought his first name was probably "Steel," to compliment his cleft chin and strong jaw line, high cheekbones, and vivid blue eyes.

I was quite happy at this point that Dr. Blake wasn't my Lady Parts doctor. I didn't think I could take that kind of pressure.

He did, however, provide the best words of encouragement I heard during my time in the hospital. "Bed rest will break the strongest person," he said. "It doesn't really matter what you've been through before, it's a totally new experience."

I nodded, my eyes filling with tears. Mostly because of what he said, but partly because he was so dazzling to look at that he hurt my eyes.

"If this doesn't break you," he said, "nothing will."

I turned this comment over in my head countless times in the days after, taking great comfort from them. They allowed me to give myself a break and concentrate a little more on the outcome, which was my precious baby Noah.

After twenty-one days, I knew I could do more. The situation totally sucked and I felt like I was going to lose my mind, but I could hang on a little bit longer.

## It Could Always Be Worse
### May 15, 2005

Alexis Everlasting, a friend of mine from high school, brought me dinner from one of my favorite restaurants. We talked, walking the one hallway I was allowed to travel.

Down at the end of this hallway was one of the two windows through which I had access to the outside world. It looked out onto the parking lot, where I could watch people come and go, oblivious to my entrapment.

Standing at the window, I watched Alexis, amazed and a little frightened. She was, after all, in a maternity ward.

A month previous, I had gone to the funeral for her stillborn baby.

I'd been nervous about going – I was obviously pregnant and unable to hide it – so I called the one person I thought would give me the best advice.

"I can't believe you've come to see me," I said. "Thank you. I don't know how you're doing it."

"Well, I've got a new perspective on life now," she said, looking out at the parking lot. "He's still here, and you can hear his heart beating," she said, nodding at my portable fetal monitor, "so, you know, it could always be worse."

I nodded, staring out at the sunny spring afternoon, watching sunlight dance among velvet leaves, listening to the steady thump of Noah's heartbeat.

## A Huge Baby
### May 19, 2005

"No lunch for you." The nurse breezed in, ready to take my vitals.

"Why not?" I asked, eyeing the toast on my breakfast tray that I'd neglected to eat.

"Doc scheduled the C-section for tonight. No food eight hours before."

"Agh!" I cried out from a contraction, which had been

happening off and on for several days. With each contraction, pain seared across my pregnant belly, sometimes leading to one of Noah's "cord episodes."

"Breathe," she said. "That's right, take a deep breath." As the pain subsided, I noted with relief that Noah's heart rate hadn't wavered. There'd been three of the "cord episodes" in the last 24 hours, which signaled that Noah was coming sooner than later.

"I'll grab you some meds to stall labor," the nurse said, heading for the door. "Remember, no food."

\*   \*   \*

The gathering in the waiting room started around dinner time with our parents and good friends, while Aaron stayed with a lady from our church. A couple of my best friends sat in the room with Jeff and me, trying to distract me from my nerves. Any hunger I'd felt had disappeared, replaced with a jumpy nausea about the delivery.

I began pacing the floor in my nervousness as nurses came in and out of the room. One handed Jeff his blue scrubs and he began putting them on.

"I'm sorry, guys," I said. "You gotta go; I don't want you to see me puke."

With hugs, they left as the anesthesiologist arrived. Soon I was wheeled in to the delivery room.

Dido played on a portable stereo while Jeff clicked pictures of the C-section and Dr. Al gave him a brief anatomy lesson.

"And here's one of her fallopian tubes," I heard Dr. Al say.

"Awesome!" Jeff answered. "That's totally sitting outside of your body, Kel!"

At that moment, I wanted to grab his intestines and pull them out of the eye of his penis, but my arms were restrained.

"Whoa, what's that?" Jeff asked.

"And that's scar tissue from Aaron's birth," Dr. Al answered. "We'll get rid of that for your wife."

"Please stop talking about my innards, I can hear you," I protested. "Please."

Their remarks continued in loud whispers, which I couldn't make out.

"Kel, here he comes," Jeff called.

I felt the pushing, pulling, and tugging – and then freedom. What was once pressing against my bladder was gone, and my middle felt wonderfully empty.

Looking to my left, I could see Noah on a scale while nurses cleaned and examined him. We heard a small cry, and they moved aside so we could take pictures of him. We could clearly see the red numbers of the scale indicating his weight.

Compared to Aaron, who was the size of a two-pound Baby Loaf of Tillamook Cheddar, Noah weighed in at a whopping four pounds!

"Whoa, he's HUGE," I said.

"Yeah, he's really big," Jeff agreed.

One of the nurses looked at us as if we were crazy. "No," she said. "Definitely not huge."

Jeff and I laughed. To us, he was a giant.

And aside from having to learn to eat, he was fine. Alive. Perfect.

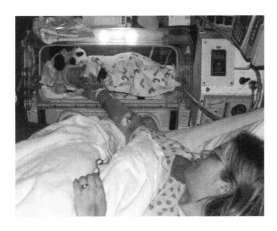

## Whoever Said "Don't Cry Over Spilled Milk" Never Had to Breastfeed
### May 27, 2005

"I can't get out of the car!" I yelled.

"Oh, dude, I'm sorry." Jeff walked around the back of the

Explorer to the open passenger door.

The gash from my C-section ached as I maneuvered out of the open car door. I slid between our car and the one right next to us. Its tires sat on the yellow line.

"It's over the line!" I grumbled.

"I know," Jeff said. "Kel, I could move our car."

"Where?" I asked. "The parking garage is full."

He shrugged as I inched my way out, taking his hand. Happy anniversary, I thought. Tears threatened, but I held them back. I'd cried every day for the last thirty-two days; I didn't want to cry today, our tenth anniversary.

Ten years, married to the same person. A milestone. We had planned a trip to Mexico, had made the reservations a year in advance, only to cancel them months before the trip.

We shuffled toward the elevator, through the skyway and maze of hallways to another elevator, and finally to the Neonatal Intensive Care Unit.

After the NICU hand-washing ritual, we headed toward Noah's Isolette, in a unit with six other babies. He slept peacefully, swaddled in a pastel blanket, a hat perched on his tiny head. Around us, monitors beeped in different pitches, what we joked was the "NICU Orchestra."

"Can you get the screens?" I asked Jeff. He nodded, looking around the unit.

A nurse approached. "What are you looking for?"

"Screens to practice breastfeeding," Jeff said.

"For Noah?"

"Yeah."

The nurse looked uncomfortable. "He seemed hungry earlier, so he's been fed. I'm sorry, we didn't know you were coming today."

Jeff and I stood in silence. We journeyed to the NICU each day, making arrangements for our oldest son to stay somewhere while we drove 15 miles to visit our youngest son. And we tried to time our visits to coincide with feedings; those were usually the only times Noah was awake.

I sat in the rocking chair Jeff pulled up behind me. I laid my head back and looked up at the ceiling, using gravity to force my tears back. I did not want to cry today – today, everything would be better.

"We can still hold him, though?" I heard Jeff ask.

"Oh, yeah, no problem," the nurse said.

Jeff picked him up, untangling the cords that measured Noah's vital signs, and laid him in my arms. I put my nose in the crease of his neck and inhaled, nuzzling his cheek next to mine.

Jeff sat across from us in another rocking chair a nurse had pulled up. Halfway through our hour visit, I offered him Noah, and left to go pump in the NICU's Pumping Room.

Usually during the first half of our daily visit I would hold Noah to my breast, surrounded by screens and usually accompanied by my husband and a nurse. After five minutes, Noah was exhausted and unable to continue breastfeeding, so they took the breast milk I'd pumped for the last twelve hours and fed it to him through a tube that ran from his nostril through his sinuses, down his throat and into his stomach.

Breastfeeding your baby while not actually having your baby with you isn't an easy task, as I knew from my experiences with Aaron when he was born. Every two to three hours I would dutifully hook up the breast pump, gather my measly ccs of milk, and refrigerate them until visiting time. I usually needed to pump while at the hospital to cover our travel time.

After my breasts had been tugged to empty, I bottled up the breast milk to take to the NICU fridge. It needed to be labeled and placed in a tray with Noah's name on it.

I carried my small cooler, with several bottles of varying levels of breast milk, to the NICU fridge. I lined up the bottles on the counter above the refrigerator.

There were six 3-ounce bottles. None were more than half-full. I opened the refrigerator and glanced inside to see several large bottles filled to the top with breast milk.

I'd seen mothers in and out of the NICU with 6-ounce bottles full of milk. I stared at mine. I'd fought hard for that milk. I wanted them to be full.

*Six half-full bottles will make three full bottles,* I said to myself, twisting the cap off the first two bottles. I turned to grab some lids.

Knocking the bottles over.

Spilling my breast milk all over the counter.

Jeff had come up behind me, ready to go. He stared. First at the puddle, then at my face.

Tears leaked, one at a time, down my face and into the puddle. *It's my tenth anniversary; I don't want to cry today.* And whoever came up with the cliché, "don't cry over spilled milk," hadn't had to pump breast milk twelve times a day for a premature infant.

"Just go ahead," Jeff said. He placed a hand on my shoulder. "I'll clean it up."

I nodded. I waited by the nearest elevator, every so often wiping my face on my sleeve.

We journeyed to the car in silence – down the elevator, across the skyway, down another elevator, and into the parking garage.

"Just cry," Jeff said in the darkness of the garage.

"I don't want to! It's our anniversary, and I have make-up on, and I don't sleep, and it's a special day, and we don't even get to do anything really special...." I blubbered, my face in my hands, standing beside our car's passenger door.

He hugged me, and I let him, pushing the side of my face against his chest. I breathed in his scent, a mix between the soap and deodorant he'd used since I first met him when I was fourteen and he was sixteen. And underneath, that slight musky smell of my adolescence that reminded me of our first high school dance and our make-out sessions, and the day we said good-bye when he went off to college. And the afternoon we got married, when the rhododendrons outside the church bloomed in brilliant fuchsia and delicate violet, and the sun warmed us as we drove away, together.

"Well," he said. "Well."

"Well, what?" I breathed in again.

"Maybe it's not about that."

"About what?" My breath hitched.

"Maybe an anniversary isn't about make-up and romance and fancy food. Maybe it's about remembering."

My tears had stopped. "Remembering what?"

"Remembering why we got married in the first place. Remembering to just be here." Stunned, I looked up at him.

"So what do we do? For our anniversary?" I asked.

"It doesn't matter. Are you ready to go?"

I shrugged. "Sure."

When we drove out of the parking garage into the sunlight, I held his hand. Sometimes, that's all you can do. It was the perfect anniversary gift.

*   *   *

Hannah and I sat in silence, the vanilla-scented candle flickering beside me. I breathed deeply, knowing that while it had been beneficial to circle around, I still hadn't traveled through the darkest part of the grief journey.

"What are you thinking?" Hannah asked. She adjusted her glasses, and brushed back a few stray hairs that had fallen out of the loose bun on the back of her head.

"The dream I had," I said. "Where I shot my dad." Hannah nodded.

"Are you sure our time isn't up yet?" I asked. We both smiled.

Cars drove in and out of the parking lot outside the window. A train whistled in the distance.

"It's time," she said. "You can do this."

"I have to do this," I said. "I have to get this all out."

It's time to nut up, I thought. Or, in my case, ovary up. With a shrug and clutching a box of tissue, I continued my story.

# SECTION THREE

## The Way, The Truth, The Life

# 16

# The Youth Pastor

## *October 1989*

**"UGH, FRESHMAN."**

I was stopped in the aisle of the yellow school bus, one hand clutching my clarinet and the other braced on the plastic green upholstery of the seat in front of me. The collar of the wool band uniform scratched my neck.

The scrawny boy in front of me scrambled to pick up his instrument from the floor while a line of freshman, including me, waited impatiently behind him. Our first half-time show, and we were nervous and excited in weather that would still top 80 degrees during the football game.

I peered around the faces of upperclassmen already seated and chatting, trying to find who'd uttered the insult against my classmates. I caught the eye of a dark-haired junior with hazel eyes. He raised his eyebrows at me as if in challenge.

It must've been him, I thought. There was nothing to do but sit in the seat across from him.

"What do you mean, 'freshman'?" I asked as I sat down.

He leaned toward me. "Exactly that. We always gotta wait for the freshman."

Unfazed, I continued the conversation with him as the bus rumbled toward the football stadium. His name was Jeff. I was fourteen, he was sixteen. We talked about Taco Bell bean burritos and farting.

It was a match made in heaven.

After our first date, he invited me to a church event called "The Body Hunt" that took place around Halloween. Essentially, there was a "body" made of straw-stuffed clothes hidden in a forested field, and whoever found it was termed the winner.

"Plus," he said when he asked me if I wanted to go, "we're going to kidnap Dave, my youth pastor."

"Okay!" I said, thinking, *what's a youth pastor?*

I had no idea. I'd only been to church a few times with a friend. We sat on creaky, metal folding chairs in a school gym where I was quickly bored. I studied the banners hanging around us – the permanent ones from the school (Go Cougars!) and the temporary ones from the church ("I am the way, the truth and the life" and "I came to give you life abundantly") that someone put up and took down when the church met each Sunday morning.

Otherwise, I hadn't read a Bible or attended a Vacation Bible School, and I wasn't too sure about this youth pastor stuff. But Jeff drove a Ford Mustang and he was really cute and older than me, so I would've gone with him to have his infected toenail removed. This was how much I liked him.

Still with no clue as to the identity of this mysterious youth pastor or why they were kidnapping him, I accompanied Jeff and some of his church friends to this Dave-person's house.

They'd gotten a hold of some handcuffs, which was best because Dave was a pretty big guy, and it took four high school dudes to hold him down and cuff him. Then they dragged him to Jeff's Mustang, where I sat in the back while they stuffed Dave into the front passenger seat.

"This is unusual," Dave said after we were introduced. I had to agree.

"Why did they kidnap you?" I asked Dave.

"This, Kelly, is a great question." He laughed.

"We wanted to make it a true Body Hunt!" Jeff said with a mock-evil laugh. "Really it's because during our last youth group meeting, Dave made us slap each other with fish."

"Gross!" I said. "Like, real fish?"

"Yep, raw fish, fresh from the grocery store."

Dave hung his head. "I figured that might cost me, but I thought you would just toilet paper my house!"

"We still might," Jeff said.

It was too early to go to The Body Hunt event without getting spotted stuffing Dave into a Honey Bucket located at the site, so we stopped by Jeff's house.

My palms started to sweat. I'd only met Jim and Evelyn once before. During that brief visit, I noticed that the house was decorated in warm colors and that Evelyn had rolls out to go with dinner.

Sourdough rolls.

Crusty on the outside, warm and fluffy on the inside, butter melting into liquid, salty nectar of the gods upon application.

When I thought of Jeff's house, I felt warm.

Helping Dave out of the car, we went inside and sat in the family room, where there was a pool table to help pass the time. A breakfast bar with stools formed a bridge between the kitchen and the family room. Dave sat, handcuffed, on one of the stools while Jeff and I played pool and joked around.

Later that night, Jeff and his friends stored Dave in a Honey Bucket as planned until somebody in the youth group found him.

They eventually let him out. Which was a good thing, because he changed my life.

## Big John, Little John
## April 1990

It turned out that the Body Hunt wasn't an isolated event. There were many more occasions that involved this youth pastor.

At a gathering around Easter that year, Dave told a story about Big John and Little John. I think it captured my attention because I'd always wanted to be a teacher, and the story was about a school teacher trying to get at the truth, along with an unexpected twist.

"In this one-room schoolhouse," Dave said, "there were about ten kids of varying ages. There were two boys named John, and the oldest they called "Big John" and the youngest they called – "

"Little John?" someone guessed.

"Correct!" Dave said and everyone laughed. "Kids came from farming families that sometimes went without, and it was during one of these tough times that the teacher noticed someone was stealing food from the other students' lunches.

So she asked them outright – Who was stealing the food? Nobody came forward.

They all got punished. Still nobody came forward. One day, she caught Big John in the act of stealing food out of another student's lunch pail. She felt terrible, because she knew how tough it was for Big John. But the other kids had seen her catch him, and she couldn't just let it go. I mean, it was stealing."

Here he paused, letting the teacher's moral dilemma sink in.

"She knew she had to punish him no matter how bad she felt. So the teacher had him choose his own switch, because the punishment was a whipping."

Made sense to me. I was no stranger to the belt. And the boy had been caught stealing, after all.

"Suddenly, Little John spoke up, sobbing. 'Teacher,' he said, 'if you must whip someone, I would like it to be me.' The teacher was shocked."

So was I. Where was Dave going with this?

"'This is Big John's punishment,' the teacher said, and raised the switch to give Big John his first lash. Before it could land, Little John cried out, 'NO! I will take the punishment for him!'"

The room was silent, and I focused all my attention on Dave.

"The teacher looked from Big John to Little John and back again. 'Someone has to take the punishment.'

Little John pushed himself in between, insisting on taking the whipping. Big John stood aside, shocked, and watched as Little John took the lashing that was meant for him while tears rolled down his face."

*Why?* I thought. *Why would someone do something like that?*

"This is what Jesus did for us," Dave finished.

A switch in my brain flipped, and in a moment I understood.

"There was a separation between people and God, and Jesus took the consequences of that separation so that we could be in relationship with him," Dave said.

I followed every word, and all that I'd heard the last few months came together in my mind.

The Way, the Truth and the Life. Jesus offers us not only life, but abundant life. We're children of God. He will not leave us nor forsake us.

Compared to the people I'd been surrounded with during my young life, Jesus sounded pretty good. Had to be better than the path I was currently traveling.

Later that night, I prayed with Jeff over the phone. I "accepted Jesus into my heart" as it was stated. I didn't know what that meant exactly, but I knew without a doubt that it had something to do with hope, which was a lot better than what I'd experienced up to that point.

## The Geek Squad
### September 1991

Rod Johnson appeared in the Advanced Placement History/Literature block the beginning of my junior year. His baseball cap accentuated his scrawny frame, brown hair, the same shade as mine, smushed underneath. The cap shaded his mellow blue eyes, tinged with some hazel, like mine. He could've been my brother.

He was a sophomore, and they didn't allow sophomores in Advanced Placement classes.

And the rest of us resented him for it. He earned the infamous nickname "Sophomore" for simply showing up. But he was okay with that, and that only made us, the mighty juniors, like him in spite of ourselves.

We were part of the "Geek Squad," the resident high school nerds, participating in activities called "The Knowledge Bowl" while other kids played basketball or got drunk at parties. We studied for our SATs and our AP exams an hour before school every day, and Rod needed a ride. I lived near him, so I volunteered.

I'd pick him up at 6:15 in the morning, my brain as foggy as the dense morning clouds. Condensation melted off my car windows, running in droplets, evaporating. I spent many late nights listening to my mother sobbing in the next room, muffled phone conversations of her desperation, pining for the monster who was my father.

"Why? Why are you leaving me?" she would sob into the phone.

I stood by my bedroom door, listening, my heart thumping in my veins, giving me a headache and making it impossible to sleep.

"You just don't understand, you could never understand," she often said to me, her nose red and sniffling. "Married for twenty-two years!"

Two decades of fighting and drunkenness and puking and cheating on her, not to mention abusing her kids. She was right, I didn't understand what she missed.

Rod would get in the car each morning and judge by the radio how I felt; music meant I felt okay, silence meant a rough night with little sleep.

"Do you want to talk about it?" he would ask, looking at me sideways, maybe wishing I'd say no. He learned more about me than he ever wanted to know.

Rod was the one who pointed out my androgyny one day, sitting with our geeky group in the cafeteria, eating lunch. My confused body image issues drove me to choose clothes at least two sizes too large. They hung from my tall frame – tee-shirts and jeans, flannel shirts, tennis shoes; from a distance, I could be male or female.

"Even your name is androgynous," he said. "Kelly can be a man's name or a woman's name."

"Not if it's K-e-l-l-i," I protested. "Then it's a girl's name."

He insisted on calling me "Pat," after the Julia Sweeney character who regularly appeared on Saturday Night Live at the time.

The nickname stuck. I loved it.

# 17

## In Which They Separate

### *Divorce Can Wait for Breakfast*
### *October 1991*

**THE PHONE RANG.** I woke, confused, and looked out my window into the gray light of dawn. It was too early for phone calls. It had to be my dad.

My dad had left for Panama in late spring, stationed for a one-year tour of duty with the Army before he was to retire. Apparently Central America isn't fond of Army families, so soldiers stationed there generally travel alone.

My mother murmured in the living room, bathed in the light of a single lamp. Her tone rose and fell, hushed because it was so early. Then it abruptly changed.

"Why?" I heard my mother moan. "Why?"

My ears perked, and my heart thumped in my chest. Her cries got louder. "What do you mean? But why? WHY?"

Alarmed, I slipped from my bed and tiptoed through my bedroom door. Goosebumps appeared on my arms, and my hair stood up on the back of my neck. I crouched in the hallway, shielded from my mom's line of sight.

"Why a divorce? What do you mean divorce? Who's Patricia? WHY?"

My mom sobbed hysterically into the phone, asking the same questions over and over again, her world crashing down around her.

I tiptoed back to bed, staring blankly at my window until I heard the beeping of my alarm. Surely he could've waited until breakfast to call?

                    *   *   *

I got up and got ready for school. Gathering my things from the dining room, my mom sat silently on the living room floor, her legs stretched out in front of her, the phone cast off to the side. One of the morning shows blared from the television. Her eyes were red-rimmed. She didn't say anything to me.

I pretended I hadn't heard anything. "Bye, Mom," I said.

She nodded.

I closed the door on the silence.

## In Which I Spill My Guts
### December 1991

My mom wanted to save their marriage. She left my younger sister and me with a family friend, and went to Panama for three weeks to be with my father.

My mom, my sister Mandy, and I sat in the living room the night she came back.

"It's no use," my mom said. "He tried to kill me. It's over."

I looked at her, not knowing just how to process the "he tried to kill me" part. I'd seen them go at it plenty of times, throwing sharp words and blunt fists, but the trying to kill her was new. Alarming.

News of their impending divorce wasn't incredibly ground-breaking information for me on the one hand. I'd asked my dad when I was twelve when he and my mom were going to get a divorce. I made sure we were in a public place so that everyone could see his face turn purple and he would have to keep his voice down. I knew that rage would probably be a consequence, but it was for most conversations. Really, I just wanted to be prepared.

Sitting with my mother now that a divorce had been decided, I made my decision.

Now was the time to tell her.

I'd tried to tell her a couple of years before. I remember lying on her bed one morning while she was getting ready for work, and I wanted so badly to tell her everything, but I don't know if I even spoke any actual words.

This time, I was using my words.

* * *

"Where was Jeff when your mom was in Panama?" Hannah asked. "Were you still dating?"

"Yeah," I said. "He was in college at the time about three hours away, so that was tough. But then there were other people around."

"What do you mean?" she asked.

I slowly released the box of tissues I'd been clutching in my hands, palms sweating. "Well, by that time I had people like Dave and Rod in my life, and youth group at church. I'd never had anything like that before. I'd always been an Army Brat."

Hannah smiled. "I like that expression."

I smiled back. "Me, too. But it's a tough childhood. I've always been from everywhere and nowhere."

## March 1984

For the first time, I would be the new kid.

I'd moved to Fort Lewis as an Army Brat when I was six weeks old, and by some fluke, we'd managed to live there until I was nine. Until then, I'd only moved from one part of the base to another, but had remained in the same school during that time, watching other kids come and go.

I walked to and from school, each morning heading straight down our street and then turning left at the corner, which was exactly halfway between our house and the school.

Single-story houses identical in every way lined both sides of the street until I reached that corner. Turning left toward school, I would pass a small hill, then a field, and finally a small patch of trees before crossing the street and arriving at my classroom.

When I was in first grade, a boy who went to afternoon kindergarten liked to play on that hill while the packs of kids from the neighborhood headed to school each morning. He called us names and threw small rocks at us, trying to hit us on our heads.

One day, I decided I'd had enough and called him names right back. I gathered a few rocks of my own and threw them at him. I bent down to gather more, and when I straightened up, a rock hit me on the left side of my forehead at the hairline.

Blood ran down my face as I walked toward school, bent over so that it wouldn't get on my coat (I wore this fabulous, fake fur zip-up number that I didn't want stained). I headed straight to the nurse's office, where she called my mom to come and pick me up.

After the visit to the doctor and subsequent stitches, the event was well-discussed over the dinner table that night. Being a very logical and concrete-thinking little girl, I answered that I was slightly closer to the school so I walked there instead of coming home.

"But how did you get hit in the head with a rock?" one of my parents asked.

"I forgot to duck," I said.

I'm not sure that I told the truth regarding the events leading up to my unfortunate injury; in fact, I'm pretty sure I skewed the facts in my favor, which would explain why my parents weren't happy about me getting hurt on the way to school.

The next morning, embarrassed but with cool new stitches in my forehead, I walked past the hill where the evil kindergartener reigned. He stood proudly, readying himself to yell at me and my pack of friends, when he looked past me and froze.

Turning around, I caught a glimpse of my dad hiding behind the thick trunk of a tree. As we continued on to school, the mom of the evil kindergartener called him inside.

When I got home from school that afternoon, the little boy came to my front door with his mom and apologized for calling me names and injuring me with a rock.

How did his mom know that her son terrorized older kids each morning from his perch? Because after my dad had been spotted, he paid her a visit to let her know what happened.

Even in first grade, I found this confusing, because he regularly yelled at me or otherwise seemed mad at me. But at the same time I was really happy, because he'd taken time to protect me.

Probably the only time.

*   *   *

It was time for us to move, not just across the United States but to another country altogether. The job of packing up my toys fell to me, and I challenged myself to see how much I could fit into each box. I had quite a few books, and this made for some heavy boxes.

Over time, though, I learned how to pack my books so that the boxes all weighed about the same and were easy to carry. Then I challenged myself to see how few boxes I could fill each time, and then how fast I could fill them.

From 1983 to 1989, we would live in seven different places. It was the beginning of all things temporary.

*     *     *

On a cloudy March day, my mom, my sister and I stumbled off the airplane in Frankfurt, Germany.

My mom had cried during the six hour flight over the Atlantic Ocean, clutching tissue and fighting claustrophobia. My sister slept in the middle seat, her head against my shoulder. I leaned against the window, staring out at the ocean rippling toward the horizon. For hours, water undulated toward a distant shore, sun reflected on its surface, nothing in its path.

When we disembarked, my dad helped us get our luggage from baggage claim, and he took us to a *gasthaus* for whatever meal we were supposed to be eating at that point in the day. I asked for water to drink, and the glass the waitress gave was full of lukewarm, bubbling liquid – carbonated water. It tasted bitter.

After *wiener schnitzel* and *pommes frites* (pork chops and fried potatoes), we headed to the apartment my father had procured "on the economy," which meant that we didn't live on the base. There were too many families and not enough living quarters, so we lived in a tiny town with narrow, winding roads, across the street from a barn. The farmers herded cows from the barn to a pasture at the end of our street in the morning and back again at night.

That first night, I fell asleep in a strange bed in our furnished apartment. I woke in the early hours of the morning, getting out of bed and feeling around in the dark for the door. I stumbled around the room in a panic, unable to find the doorknob. Unable to get out.

Finally I staggered into the hall, and made my way through the dark into the kitchen. I sat at the cold Formica table with its metal border and clutched a kitchen towel. The chair creaked as I silently cried, rocking back and forth.

The rest of the furniture was old and heavily brocaded. There were turquoise side chairs covered in stitched flowers in the living room. The wheels on the bottom allowed them to roll around on the thick, olive green shag carpet, and they tilted back like office chairs.

As weeks passed, I would avoid these chairs as well as the rest of the house. I hid in my room, trying to avoid the random pornography on the television, or the sight of my father leaned back in one of the chairs, exposing himself and smirking at me.

I was relieved to move late that summer, to live on base and make friends with other American kids (my German wasn't very good). I thought – hoped – my dad's behavior would stop.

It only intensified.

## December 1984

The company parties on the base were frequent and legendary. Far from home and family, the American soldiers and their spouses drank. A lot.

Families gathered this Christmas at the base skating rink. The kids skated around to popular songs like "Maneater" and danced the "Hokey Pokey," but avoided the Couples' Skate. The adults consumed copious amounts of different forms of alcohol, gathering around the edge of the skating rink and spilling out the front door into the parking lot.

At one point early in the evening, the lights brightened and the DJ played a fanfare. A spotlight trained on my dad dressed as Santa, carrying a large velvet bag bulging with toys.

At the urging of the crowd, all of the kids sat on "Santa's" lap. His bleary eyes were the only part of his face that showed. The smell of alcohol floated off him in waves. I perched uncomfortably on his lap and smiled while my mom's camera snapped the picture, and then I quickly escaped.

After parties like this, my mom or dad, both intoxicated, drove us home, weaving and over-correcting, driving drunk. I crouched in the back seat, taking note of the close calls and forgetting to breathe until we arrived home.

The fun wouldn't end there, though. Additional drunken activity involved yelling and scuffling until the police showed up. I would sneak to my sister's room, and we would huddle in the space between her bed and the wall while I prayed nobody would come in and find us.

If not yelling or scuffling, one or both of my parents often spent the early morning hours vomiting loudly in the apartment's only bathroom. Covering my head with a pillow, I fought panic, unable to slow my heartbeat.

My dad wasn't what you would call a quiet puker. It sounded like his guts were coming out and he was going to die.

During the middle of one particular night, my dad opened my door and crept into my room. He sat on the edge of my bed for awhile.

My heart thumped. This could not be good.

*Pretend to sleep*, a little voice whispered in my head. A tiny voice of warning that echoed in my brain.

I obeyed.

The silence dragged on as he seemed to sit there for hours. I hardly breathed, waiting.

He grabbed my hand, dragging it over to his lap. *MOVE!* the voice yelled, sudden, unmistakable.

I obeyed again, pretending as if I was shifting in my sleep. I turned over and faced the window.

Slowly – so slowly – he got up, closing my door gently behind him.

I stared into the darkness.

\*    \*    \*

My cousin, who was ten years older than me, had married an Army Captain and moved to a nearby base. Family was difficult to come by, and we were happy to join her, her husband and her toddler for Christmas that year.

Apartments on base were small, and sleeping arrangements were cramped. My parents slept on an air mattress on the floor, while my sister and I slept on the couches on either side.

I woke with my shirt pulled up to my armpits. My dad stared at my chest, transfixed.

My brain tweaked.

I felt it. It was a definite shutting down in an instant, like when you flip a light switch – suddenly, the room is either light or dark in a moment, and everything is different.

I pulled my shirt down and rolled over.

Later, he sat me on his lap while others went about making breakfast. "This morning is not something we need to tell anyone," he said.

To be honest, I don't know what I said, if anything. My brain was "off."

"Don't tell anyone," he repeated.

\* \* \*

"So the Post-traumatic stress disorder around Christmas is pretty clear now," Hannah said.

"Right? It makes all kinds of sense now, why for years I've gotten really sick right around Christmas time," I said.

## Bathroom Mirror

### 1985

"I'll be back soon," my mom shut the door behind her. I grabbed my copy of Nancy Drew from the coffee table and headed to my room. Close to the end, I was anxious to finish it and begin another one.

Propped against the headboard, I drowned in the story, unaware of anything happening outside my bedroom door. My glasses, easily a quarter-inch thick, slid down a nose decorated with newly clogged pores. I pushed them up automatically every few minutes.

Footsteps lumbered down the hall toward my bedroom door. I stiffened. My eyes moved over the page, though I failed to comprehend the words. The door opened against my will. I didn't look up.

"Time to get ready for bed," my dad growled, heading for the couch where he'd stashed his choice of alcohol for the evening. That night, he meant to conquer a twelve pack of cheap beer.

"OK," I mumbled, pretending to read.

I sighed, remembering that I had to take a shower before bed. I ran my fingers through my thick, honey-colored hair. It fell back to my shoulders, dull and greasy from the onslaught of puberty and lack of applied shampoo.

My mom had recently told me that I needed to shower every day, I'm no longer a little girl. I'd wondered at the time what getting older had to do with a daily showering ritual. Then I saw the video at school – the one where they separate the boys and girls and talk about periods and body odor and wet dreams. In fifth grade, this is heady stuff, much juicier than the typical rumors running through circles of girls cloistered around cafeteria tables at lunch. That the information was true made it more fascinating.

From my dresser drawer, I grabbed my nightgown and the stupid flowered panties my mom insisted on buying. I wondered when I'd have a training bra in the same drawer; I'd heard about those after the infamous video. Maybe I could get more "grown up" underwear to go with it.

The bathroom, located at the back of the house, was two doors down on the left from my room. Far from the living room. I didn't have to pass near it, but I hurried anyway. The television droned as my dad let out a beer-induced belch.

There was only one bathroom in the house, which added to the importance of my showering in the evening – there wasn't enough time for all of us to get ready in the morning. I didn't agree that I needed to shower every night – I'd been sniffing my armpits for days and still hadn't smelled anything but my skin. *Maybe the body odor will just happen out of the blue.* It can't hurt to be prepared.

From the door, the flowered shower curtain hung in front of the tub. Pastel blues and pinks covered every corner of the bathroom – one blue rug and one pink rug, blue flowers, pink flowers, blue bathmat, blue and pink décor lining the shelf below the mirror. The white of the walls and the beige of the laundry hamper provide the only visual escape from the pastel assault.

The hamper could hardly contain anything at all; the broken plastic at the top edge jutted out from years of use, threatening to scratch hasty hands. It stood almost to my chest, with slats along each face. The slats were sufficiently wide enough to stick a hand through and turn it back and forth. Some of the openings could accommodate two hands, the plastic between them broken long before.

I noticed the toilet had been freshly scrubbed; my younger sister's job. My job was cleaning the tub. At least twice a week. Over and over again. Until there was no residue of soap or cleaner. Until I could eat out of it.

"Use a little elbow grease! Don't think you're going to be done anytime soon!" My mom would harshly repeat.

I shuddered, vowing to someday never clean a tub again.

I began to undress, at first throwing my "play" clothes on the floor. I didn't believe in washing clothes daily; they lose their comfort, get all stiff, and then you have to break them in again. Jeans are the worst for that.

My current pair of pants (just broken in) showed evidence of the crumbly, cheesy chips I ate at lunch. They must be washed, I regretfully decided.

I lifted the lid of the hamper and dropped my clothes inside.

"Push those clothes down as far as you can! There's hardly any clothes in there as it is! Make sure we can get a full load in there!" My mom's voice reminded me.

Obeying the voice, I stuck my arm into the laundry basket and pushed down firmly. My hand jammed against a hard, metal object.

Confused, I removed shirts and shifted stinky socks around. I saw the top of a video camera. Facing the bathtub. The lens fit perfectly between two slats in the hamper.

It was recording.

I stared at the red light. Goose pimples spread across my flesh. I put my clothes back on, moving quickly, and opened the bathroom door.

"Dad?" I called.

"What?!" he yelled over the noise of the television.

"There's something in the hamper," I began, but he was already on his way.

He passed me in the doorway, didn't look at me. He smirked as he gathered up the video camera, turned, and left the bathroom without a word.

I closed the door behind him. Silently, I stared at all that pink and blue as my brain struggled to comprehend.

I began to undress again, haltingly, slowly. I saw myself in the bathroom mirror over the sink, my brow furrowed and my frown, my eyes blank.

As I stared in the mirror, I made a decision. As soon as I possibly could, I had to get out, to get away from them. The only way was to do well in school so I could go to college and then I would be a teacher. Then everything would be alright.

I guess I've always been a planner.

I studied my reflection. My arms and legs dangled awkwardly from a potato-shaped trunk that hadn't yet caught up with my recent growth spurt. Baby fat gathered at my waist and in my face. My breast buds had begun to peak noticeably. I noticed fuzzy hair where there was once none.

My eyes narrowed as I stared.

I faced the tub and turned the faucet to hot. Only hot. The steam from the shower would fog the mirror.

*     *     *

"Why did you decide to be a teacher?" asked Hannah.

"That's a funny story, actually," I said with a smile.

"Good, I could use it." Hannah got up from the couch with a groan. "Too much *krav maga* this morning," she remarked and crossed the room to her desk. It was neat and tidy – alarmingly so to someone like me, who locates important documents based on where piles are placed around the house.

She opened a drawer and rummaged around. "A-ha!" A bag of individually wrapped chocolate candy landed in my lap. Heaven.

"Where's yours?" I asked, opening the bag.

"Ha ha," she said, passing by my chair to grab a handful. "You looked like you could use some temporary comfort." Settling back into the couch cushions across from me, she asked, "Do you know why I love *krav maga*?"

I shook my head as silky chocolate melted on my tongue. The joy of the velvety comfort traveled deep into the center of my brain. "I don't even know what *krav maga* is."

"It's a form of martial arts from Israel. 'Krav maga' means "Contact Combat." So you get right in the thick of it," she said, unwrapping a piece of chocolate and popping it into her mouth.

"Nobody tells me that I have to hold back, I hit as hard as I can, charge as hard as I can, until I crap my pants or throw up – or both."

My mouth hung open, the latest piece of chocolate almost landing in my lap. "Huh?"

Hannah nodded. "Yep, I was doing this kickbox-punch combination super hard in class, and my stomach rumbled. Ten seconds later, I projectile vomited and pooped my pants at the same time."

I stared, mouth open, imagining the scene. Punching bags hanging from the ceiling, people grunting and punching and kicking, the smell of gym socks and plastic mats...and poop.

I moved the bag of chocolate from my lap to the table next to my chair. The color and the texture of the chocolate would not be reconciled with the images in my brain.

She grinned with triumph and pride. "I spewed everything I'd eaten since the third grade. I was on my hands and knees, covered in sweat and vomit and poop, and you know what I heard?"

I shook my head, mouth still hanging open. I cleared my throat. "Laughter?" I asked, horrified.

"Nope. Applause!"

"What?"

"They were gathered around, all the class regulars."

"An appropriate distance away, I imagine," I said.

She inclined her head in agreement. "They clapped and whistled and someone yelled, 'YAAAAAY! You've popped your cherry!'"

I smiled, chuckling. "Seriously?"

"Yes!"

"And then what?" I asked.

"My instructor handed me a spray bottle of bleach and a towel."

"Yeah, I'm not going to take a *krav maga* class," I said.

"So now that you know that about me," Hannah said, "please continue. Why did you want to become a teacher? You said it would be a funny story."

## *Mrs. Bottiggi*
## *November 1985*

The top floor of the double-decker bus swayed with the effort of staying upright while navigating the narrow curves of the German village. My stomach fought to keep the contents of my breakfast safely inside my body, while news arrived that someone had lost his or hers down below. I silently gave thanks that I wasn't there to take in the stench and promptly puke in sympathy.

My fifth-grade teacher, Mrs. Bottiggi, staggered to the stairs leading down to the main deck. I heard snippets of the bus driver's German mingled with the voices of chaperones trying to manage the mess.

"Don't come down," one of them told her. "We've got it taken care of."

Mrs. Bottiggi sighed and turned to go back to her seat, carefully grabbing the tops of the seats as she went. Her four-inch heels provided a challenge to her balance. Her tan raincoat, covering a purple and fuchsia pantsuit, swished against the sides of the seats. Her reading glasses dangled at her ample chest from a sparkly gold chain.

Mrs. Bottiggi was the ultimate of what my friends and I would later term a 1980s "pretty lady." Beautifully coiffed, platinum blonde hair swirled around the back of her head into a carefully constructed bun. Trailing pleasantly aromatic perfume, she swished when she walked, indicating daily panty hose – dress, skirt, or pants. Her make-up impeccably matched the jeweled tones of her clothes.

"Who was it?" one of the chaperones sitting near us asked Mrs. Bottiggi.

"I don't know, but I hope the driver doesn't yell at me. My German's not too sharp." Her laugh was husky and booming.

We were on another one of our ill-fated field-trips. On our last one, visiting the local branch of the Army newspaper, I'd been hit in the mouth with a tennis ball while playing catch. On the one before that, we'd misunderstood the bus driver when he told us where to meet the bus when we finished at the museum. We wandered around for an hour before we found the bus, and then the driver did yell, but none of us knew much German, so at least we were spared the content.

As Army brats, we were products of the Federal Government's commitment to public education for military dependents. Since we were in a foreign country, our fifth-grade class took advantage of the cultural and educational opportunities around us.

Today's field-trip was touring centuries-old castles and churches in our area. We had just eaten lunch and were winding down our field-trip with our last stop.

The bus dropped us off at an iron gate, the entrance to the church's graveyard. Huddled under umbrellas, we shuffled through damp leaves, surrounded by moss-covered headstones. We brushed our fingers along engravings worn down by decades of abuse from the elements. My imagination spun fantasies about who lay in the ground and what their lives may have been like. I recalled the ghost stories I'd read about graveyard specters and felt a shiver, accentuated by the rain pounding my umbrella and soaking my feet.

The sagging stone church sat in a clearing in the center of the graveyard. The chaperones and Mrs. Bottiggi split our group into two lines, one that would start in the church, and one that would start by viewing the underground baptismal pool.

Our leader carried a lantern and sported a mustache that arched down until it met his chin. It moved up and down with each heavily-accented word.

"At the bottom of these stairs is a pool of vater," he began. He explained that the purpose of the pool was for the people of the village to get baptized.

"And no one," he pointed out, "has used this pool in a long, long time."

"How long?" a classmate blurted.

"A long, long time. Many years. Ve vill go down the stairs to view the pool. The stairs are narrow, so go down, see the pool, and turn around and come back up," he continued, leading us to a set of stone steps that spiraled into darkness.

He gestured to me, saying, "Vhy don't you lead us down?"

I stared at him dumbly. "But vhat about lights?" I inadvertently said a "v" instead of a "w". Some kids laughed. I blushed.

He seemed not to notice. "I have the lantern," he explained. "I vill be in the middle of the line so everyone has light."

Having little experience with lantern light, I headed for the steps, into a tangible darkness. My feet slipped on the stairs slimy with moss. I slowly took one step at a time, left foot, then right foot. Left foot, right foot.

Several stairs down, I sensed a circle of dim light behind me. My fingers brushed the slick walls. The stairs seemed to go on forever. The silent processional of students behind me held their collective breath.

"A few more," our tour guide called out.

My left foot slipped, a feet-in-the-air, butt-on-the-ground kind of fall. I imagined a bone cracking on the unforgiving steps below me.

Instead, I sank into the baptismal pool with a fantastic splash. Limbs crashing around, I got my bearings and stood in a pool of water waist-high.

The narrow stone corridor echoed with feet scrambling and fifth-graders screaming.

*"AAAAHHHHHHHH,"* was all I could yell, over and over.

The lantern light disappeared up the stairwell, and then reappeared and came closer.

"Hello?" our tour guide called. "Come up! Come up!"

I turned around in circles and felt for the stairs, shivering with fright and cold. The tour guide came down with the lantern and clutched my arm, helping to pull me out of the pool and up the spiral stairs to the courtyard, where I stood, soaked to the bone, surrounded by my gawking classmates.

"Are you all right?" Mrs. Bottiggi shrieked and clacked out of the church on her high heels, her raincoat unbuttoned and swaying around her.

I nodded and shivered, unnecessarily covered by someone's umbrella. She looked me up and down with a worried frown, fuchsia lips pursed.

"Marilyn," she called to a chaperone, "come with me. Everyone else line up in two lines."

She conferred with the tour guides and then came over to me, Marilyn in tow. "Let's go," she directed, gently leading me toward the campground style bathrooms located next to the church.

In the room marked *"Damen,"* we stood between two rickety stalls and a stained sink. There was no mirror, nor was there heat.

Mrs. Bottiggi looked at Marilyn and me and explained her plan. We agreed on its viability, and I entered one stall while Mrs. Bottiggi entered the other. Marilyn stood outside the doors to assist.

I tugged my wet jeans over my soaked shoes and socks. I slid those and my tee-shirt and bra underneath the stall door and into Marilyn's waiting hands. I could hear Mrs. Bottiggi in the stall next to me, and could see the purple pantsuit as she handed it to me under the stall wall.

"Got it," I said, and put on the pantsuit. It was baggy, especially the chest.

I came out of the stall, struggling with the purple buttons. A fuchsia belt hugged my waist.

Marilyn and I watched as Mrs. Bottiggi's stall door opened and she appeared wearing her raincoat, buttoned from neck to calf. She had also affixed her belt for good measure.

"With these pantyhose and shoes, no one will need to know," she smiled, hair and makeup still perfect.

I smiled back, and the three of us exited the bathroom, carrying my clothes.

My mom waited for us as we arrived back at school. We posed for pictures, Mrs. Bottiggi's arm around me and her purple pantsuit. Her perfume filled my nose. I felt warm. More than anything, I wanted to be like her.

Mrs. Bottiggi didn't know it, but she'd saved me, and not just from the baptismal pool. I'd found my way out, away from my parents. I would go to college, and I knew exactly what I would be.

I wanted to be a teacher.

# 18

# In Which He is Arrested

## January 1992

"I TALKED WITH your dad today," my mom said quietly, glancing out the window of the restaurant. It was one of her favorite places, and I thought of it as the "Diner of Despair." When we met there, it was never good news.

"Really?" I asked. Internally, I cringed.

"He's going back to Patricia." She spat out 'Patricia' and rolled her eyes.

I stared down at a small crack in the table. "Have they found out if he's the father of her kids?" I asked.

"No, and they probably won't," she answered sharply, slouching in the leather booth. She crossed her arms, and her hard stare stabbed the window.

"What about the police?" I asked. I'd talked with a detective on the military base within a few days of sharing my experiences with my mom. I explained my story and answered questions, and now we were in a holding pattern.

Her stare stabbed me this time. "We can't do anything until he comes back in May."

## May 1992

My mom, my sister, and I again met at the Diner of Despair.

"Good news," my mom said. "We can all go home." She had lost a lot of weight in the spring, and her face was sunken and hard with anger; her eyes glinted like two small pebbles.

The three of us had separated upon my dad's return from Panama. The authorities considered him violent and advised us to stay away from our house. I'd stayed with Jeff's parents for a few nights, while Jeff was still away at college.

"What happened?" I asked.

"He flew in, and they met him at the gate," she said. "They took him away in handcuffs."

"Then what?"

"They questioned him, held him for awhile. He didn't confess, and there was nothing they could do," she said. "But he's not coming back."

I sat, numb from the effort of trying to process the anti-climactic nature of his release. I couldn't believe they could just let him go. My stomach sank, and I felt slightly ill. How could they know for sure we'd be safe at home?

He's not coming back? I wasn't so sure I could believe that.

# 19

## In Which They Get Back Together

### *July 22, 1992*

**ON A WARM,** sunny July evening, I joked and laughed with my friends, soaked from water games we'd just played at Wednesday night youth group.

"Hey, Kel," Dave called across the field. "They need you in the church office."

I waved and jogged over to the church, greeted by a blast from the air conditioning. I shivered from the change in temperature on my damp clothing and saw my mom in the office area with the pastor of the church. She was crying, her eyes a watery red, a tissue clutched in her hand.

"What happened?" I asked. My stomach flipped. "Grandma and Grandpa were in an accident, a car accident," she said. "Grandma's in a coma, and Grandpa's dead." She choked out the last part of the sentence.

"I have to say goodbye," I said, turning to go back outside.

"They already know," she said. "We have to go; we're leaving in the morning."

* * *

As we drove up to the house, I noticed lights on in the living room and the bedrooms, along with my dad's car in the driveway.

"Is Dad here?" I asked.

"Yes," my mom said, shutting off the car. "He's driving us to California."

"Wha–?" I started.

"Look, he knew your Grandpa for years; he was like a father to your dad." She grabbed the keys from the ignition. "Let's go."

I struggled to close my mouth, wide open from shock. Dazed, I got out of the car and stumbled through the front door.

My dad sat on the couch, watching television as if he'd never left, guzzling a can of beer.

I didn't acknowledge him as I passed him, heading for the kitchen. Opening the refrigerator, I saw bottles of vodka and a variety of malt beverages.

Rage filled my chest. My heart raced. I felt like it would explode.

"I need you to pack," my mom said, following me into the kitchen.

I slammed the refrigerator door, pushing by her as I went to my room. My whole body shook as I grabbed clothes and stuffed them into a duffel bag. I could hear the television droning, and I felt lost in the confusion, numb with powerlessness while making sure to pack underwear and my book light.

Suddenly I felt very tired, and I stopped to lie down on my bed. Later I startled awake, feeling like it'd been a nightmare. My grandpa wasn't dead, and my dad wasn't in the living room. My stomach rumbled, and I saw myself reflected in the darkness of my bedroom window.

I couldn't go. I couldn't do this.

On silent feet, I padded to the kitchen to grab something to eat and avoid speaking with anyone.

"Did you pack?" my mother said, sneaking up behind me as I reached for a banana lying on the counter. "We're leaving at oh-dark-thirty."

My body tensed. How could she be so casual? I whirled around to face my mother.

"NO!" I yelled. "I'M NOT GOING."

I grabbed her car keys off the counter and ran out the front door, heading to the only place I could think of going.

"Get back here!" I heard her yell as I slammed the car in reverse and peeled out of the driveway.

\*   \*   \*

Jeff's house was dark, illuminated by a single porch light. I sat in the driveway, wondering how this could've happened. How he could be back, how she could allow it. Her frequent outings and late nights suddenly made sense, and I felt like a fool for not seeing it – she must've been seeing him over the last couple of months, hiding it from me.

And my only grandfather had died, and my grandmother might soon follow. How could I not go? What could I do?

Overwhelmed, I used the key I still carried from when I'd stayed there briefly in May, and I gently turned it at the front door.

I felt my way in the darkness, down the hallway to Jeff's room. Home from college for the summer, his parents hadn't yet turned his boyhood room into a guest room.

Fortunately, I saw that his parent's bedroom door was closed and sighed with relief. Chances were good that they'd never know I'd been here.

"Jeff," I whispered, tapping him on the shoulder. "Jeff!"

"Wha–?"

"Shh!" I said. "I have to go to California in a few hours."

"Your grandpa?" he asked, groggy and confused.

"Yeah," I whispered. "Just wanted to say goodbye."

He woke up a little more. "When will you be back?"

"I don't know," I said. I had no energy to explain all that was going on.

"I love you," he said as we hugged goodbye. "Call me."

I nodded, turning to leave in the silence and darkness.

*   *   *

Only the porch light shone as I arrived home. Packed suitcases belonging to my parents and sister Mandy sat by the front door.

I picked my way as quietly as I could through the dark house to my bedroom. Nobody was awake, or at least nobody was up.

The next morning, my own bag was packed and ready to go.

Nobody said a word about the night before.

\* \* \*

## Crinkle, Crinkle

I stood at the side of my Grandpa's coffin, staring at his face bright with makeup. His cheeks, the color of ripe peaches, were gaunt, and his eyes were closed.

I studied his face, my brain parched like the desert in the middle of a summer day. There were no thoughts, as there had been no sleep on the drive from our home in Washington to central California or after.

I'd done my best to avoid my dad at all costs. Always slightly drunk and fully angry, he liked to cause scenes, which I couldn't avoid. We ate breakfast the first morning of our trip in a roadside chain restaurant, and he decided he didn't like the food.

"This is too salty! What do you call this shit?" He yelled at the waitress. He threw his fork, and it rattled against his plate.

Even as a seventeen-year-old, I hunkered down farther into the booth, not looking, not eating, not breathing.

Now I ran my fingers over my grandpa's shirt, a starched white button down instead of his typical plaid, Western style with snaps. *Crinkle, crinkle.*

The funeral director stood at the head of the coffin. Looking up at him, I asked, "Why does he *crinkle*?"

His discomfort was immediately apparent. He cleared his throat and looked into the distance. "Well, they drained his bodily fluids, and then filled his body with embalming fluid."

"Uh huh," I said. Even in my numbness, I was entertained, feeling like I'd broached a forbidden subject.

He looked at me a long moment, as if I was supposed to understand something subtle, something he didn't want to say. I stared him down, willing him to explain.

"Then they enclose the body in plastic..." he shifted, "...so it doesn't leak."

"Ah," I said. Made sense to me. I wanted to laugh out loud.

After a last look at my grandpa, I turned to find a seat for the funeral, far away from my father.

* * *

## A Trunk Full of Vodka Bottles

I'm not quite sure how I found out that my mother and father were getting back together.

Not part of an extended family who likes to talk frankly about anything, I probably heard it from one of my cousins in a whispered conversation behind the barn (everyone who's grown up on a farm knows that the only real privacy is behind the barn).

My grandmother's house buzzed with activity in the days before and after my grandpa's funeral. Extended family members gathered in groups. I found my mother outside at one of the picnic tables in my grandmother's front yard. For once, my father wasn't sitting with her.

"Mom, you can't be serious," I said.

She ignored me, pretending to participate in a conversation at the far end of the table.

"You can't get back together with him," I tried again. She refused to look at me, let alone speak to me. As I was on my third day without sleep, I felt a strange combination of numbness and despair.

One of my aunts nudged me. "Come here," she said. Not in any shape to argue, I stumbled after her. I passed by another group talking about my father's presence and his "bottles of vodka in the trunk." I supposed he'd come prepared.

"You need to get some sleep," my aunt said, digging around in her purse. "This will help."

She handed me a little blue pill as we stood by the kitchen sink, along with a glass filled with water.

I nodded, unable to think.

I woke up about eighteen hours later, and it was time to head home.

* * *

"Valium!" Hannah said. "That's intense."

I nodded. My fingers played with the plastic bag of chocolate still sitting on my lap. It crinkled as I folded and unfolded it.

"What did you think was going to happen?" she asked.

I shrugged. "I had a plan of sorts. I was going to protect my sister somehow, but my brain was too fuzzy to think logically. I just knew that my sister and I couldn't stay in the same house with my parents."

Hannah nodded.

"It turns out, though, that I didn't have to worry about it. At least, not the way I thought I would."

# 20

# Moving On, But Not From Grief

## A Place to Stay

### August 1992

"WE HAVE TO LEAVE," my mom stated.

We'd been home only a couple of weeks. After driving back from California, I stayed away from home as much as possible, since my mom and dad had decided to get back together. There was never any conversation or announcement – he had simply moved back in.

It hadn't gone well. Bruises covered her arms and neck. We sat, once again, at the Diner of Despair. I don't think my mother ate anywhere else.

"He beat me up, took everything. So I'm taking your sister, and we're moving to California."

I digested the words for a moment, and noticed that I wasn't involved in this plan. At fourteen years old, my sister Mandy didn't have a choice. I didn't know if she wanted to go to California, but it was clear that her feelings didn't matter.

I wasn't sure what to do about my sister. Should I call someone to intervene? Should I try and take her in? I was seventeen with no place to go, with little in the way of options.

My mother continued, breaking into my thoughts. "Your grandmother needs a lot of help right now, she needs someone to take care of her. I'm going to do that."

I nodded. My grandmother had survived the car accident and the resulting coma but had suffered many injuries. I'd heard that she would need a hospital bed at home in order to recover, along with assistance.

"When's this happening?" I asked, getting up to leave for my shift at the fast-food restaurant where I worked.

Survival instinct had kicked in, with a desire to solve my problem of finding a place to live.

"Two weeks. And you need to finish your senior year of high school. So you need to find a place to live."

I nodded again, my brain whirling with possibilities. "I have to go to work," I said.

My mom nodded, absently rubbing the bruises on her arms.

I walked out in a daze. Where would I stay? I had a pretty good idea about where to start.

*   *   *

Warmth greeted me as I opened the front door, and I realized how exhausted I was after my grease-filled, eight-hour shift at the fast-food restaurant.

"Hi, Scooter!" Jim yelled as I walked through the dark kitchen and into the brightly lit living room.

I walked down the carpeted step between the two recliners and bent to give him a hug. He dug into a new bag of peanut M&Ms as I walked around his chair and stretched out on the expanse of brown carpet. Evening sunlight poured in from the tall windows.

Jim turned off the noisy television. "So, how was your trip, Kiddo?"

"As well as could be expected, I suppose."

"Well," he began, "it's obvious you want to talk about something, so let's just take care of business."

I smiled – "take care of business" was one of his consistent philosophies.

"Well, I called earlier because I wanted to tell you that my dad's gone again and my mom and sister are moving to California. I need a place to live if I'm going to stay for my senior year, and I want, well, I want to live here." My palms were sweating, and I was working hard to keep my voice from trembling.

He pursed his lips, bunching together his thick brown mustache. He studied me for a moment. "When is this all happening?"

"About two weeks." I smiled, because if I didn't, I would cry.

He nodded. "Well," he began slowly, "I don't see a problem with it, as long as you do all the women's work around here. We've got plenty," he paused for effect. "Dishes, laundry...."

"Clean toilets?" I couldn't help but grin.

"Yeah! And of course, women belong in the kitchen, so that's probably where you'll spend most of your time. And you will, of course, learn how to cook. We don't have any freeloaders in my house."

He tried to remain serious through this speech, leaning as far back as he could in his recliner. Since business was taken care of, we could joke.

I offered a weak smile, too tired to play the feminist in our usual banter. He already knew that I despise cooking, especially after burning instant pudding. My eyes filled with tears as I finally had time to sit and think about the changes that were about to happen.

The moment passed, and we discussed the rules of the household – curfew, chores, dinner time – and what would be expected of me.

"You know that you'll be 'Baby Kelly' now, don't you?" he asked, eyebrow cocked.

I shrugged, grinning. I would, after all, officially be the youngest.

I pulled myself up from the floor. As I walked by his chair, I couldn't resist poking him in the ribs.

I walked down the hallway, decorated with pictures of Jim, Evelyn, Steve, and Jeff – and soon, me – to the bedroom that would become mine in the next two weeks.

It was clean and beige, ready for my few boxes and collection of androgynous flannel shirts. Surveying the room, I solved the most important problem – I imagined where I would put my books.

\* \* \*

I was working the drive-thru window the next day when my dad drove through my line.

In my car.

It was stuffed full of black garbage bags. I could see our computer crammed in the back seat.

"Can you talk?" he shouted through the car's open window.

I shook my head.

He nodded and drove away. That was the last time I saw him.

## June 1993

It was a balmy June night – a couple of days before high school graduation – when Rod, me, and the rest of the Geek Squad gathered after we'd crashed graduation parties and stolen orange street cones from road construction sites.

We'd ended up at Alexis's house, playing pool inside and Frisbee outside. Street lamps reflected off the Frisbee, making it easier to see the swirling disk in the dark. Soon Rod and I were the only ones outside. We rested on the curb, watching the stars and the breeze rustle summer leaves. Sitting side-by-side, we talked in the security of darkness.

"I've never told anyone this before," I said.

"Yeah?"

"Sometimes I think...I don't think I can go on."

"What do you mean? Like suicide?" he asked.

"Yeah," I answered my voice quiet and small, as far away as the stars.

The silence stretched, and I looked over at him out of the corner of my eye. He stared at the ground, forehead creased and mouth tight.

"I can't believe after all this, after you've made it this far, you would say that," he said. "It's so...so selfish!"

"I know," I said, throwing loose rocks into the road. I turned and looked into the windows of Alexis's house, watching our friends play pool and drink soda and eat chips, unaware.

I had meant what I said. I did think about it. I no longer had the luxury of childhood innocence. But I also felt comforted, like if someone like Rod would be mad at me for even thinking about it, then maybe I was worth something, lovable.

"Never again, then," I said.

His face relaxed. "Good."

We stood, and I kicked the gravel awkwardly, staring at the sky and smelling the sun in the dirt.

"Let's go in," Rod said.

I nodded. As I turned we hugged, sealing my promise.

## College
### August 1993

Every available space in the Chevy Citation II was crammed with boxes and duffel bags. The stuff was mine, the car provided the previous summer by Jim and Evelyn.

I was destined to be the new kid again. My boxes and I were headed off to college a couple of hours away. It was the beginning of a new life.

My senior year of high school, I applied to about five colleges along with Financial Aid. Though I lived with Jim and Evelyn, I was essentially on my own. I had no money, so I asked God to tell me where to go to college based on how much financial assistance each college was willing to give me. The one that gave me the most would be the winner.

I received acceptance letters accompanied by financial statements that included several thousands of dollars worth of loans I would have to carry.

Except for one.

Warner Pacific College in Portland, Oregon offered me a full-ride scholarship. Finally, I was on my way to becoming a teacher, leaving the rest behind.

# 21

## Awkward Grief

### *A Grief Removed?*

### *Fall 1996*

**THE LID TO THE COFFIN** gaped an inch, enough to squeeze my fingertips against it and lift.

"Coffin" seemed a fancy word for the plywood box that held Michelle. It sat on a table at the far end of the room in front of rows of metal folding chairs.

"Should we...?" Alexis whispered.

I shrugged, my fingers against the gap.

If I'd known what was going to happen next, I would've said, "No."

\* \* \*

I got a call from Alexis early that morning. I was surprised to hear her voice. We'd grown to be pretty good friends in high school, but I hadn't really talked with her the past few years since we were attending separate colleges.

"It's not good," Alexis said. "Rachel wanted me to call you." Rachel was a mutual friend from high school.

"What's up?"

"Michelle has – well, she's dead," she said. Michelle was Rachel's younger sister.

"I'll be there as soon as I can," I said.

When I arrived, I found Rachel surrounded by family members. There wasn't much to say after I hugged her.

I watched as visitors tromped in and out, sharing, eating, crying, and laughing. Old friends came in to surprised "Hellos", hugs, and pats on their backs. We'd engage in excited conversation, catching up on school (college for most of us), jobs, families, and happenings.

Awkward silence followed. Uncomfortable, furtive looks. Somehow it would hit us all at once – why we were here in the first place. The guilt of the conversation and the laughter led to tears for most people.

For me, not so much. I'd always been a joker, using humor to diffuse difficult situations. But this was just too terrible. I simply didn't know what to do.

I stationed myself on the couch, flipping through a cookbook I found on the coffee table. A page of the cookbook was dog-eared, bent at the top. The folded triangle flapped, almost unattached. Chocolate chip cookies, of course – Michelle's specialty.

"That was Michelle's favorite recipe," I heard Mrs. Butler – Rachel and Michelle's mom – say over my right shoulder. She came over and caressed the page.

I froze, wanting to slam the cookbook closed.

She looked at me, eyes gleaming, her lips trembling in a closed-mouthed smile. I stared back at her, unable to speak. Unable to breathe.

She turned away, sobbing, down the hallway to her room.

Damn it! I thought.

I started to follow her and instead attacked Alexis as she exited the bathroom.

"I gotta get out of here," I said.

She nodded. We'd been there since mid-morning, and it neared dinnertime.

"The viewing's not until 7:00, so we've got some time," she said. "Let me get my coat."

Making sure Rachel would be okay, we jumped into Alexis's car and headed for town. We drove around for a while, deciding to stop at a Christian bookstore. We wanted to find something that might make things all right.

"Are they Christians?" I asked as we got out of the car.

"They're Catholic – is that the same thing?" Alexis asked.

We shrugged at each other. "Does it really matter?" I asked.

We went inside. An hour later we came out, disappointed. Nothing was going to make this okay.

We drove around, reluctantly heading toward the viewing.

*　*　*

We were late.

The scene was out of a low-budget horror flick. The funeral home was a double-wide trailer that sat on the edge of a cemetery. Rain hung in misty sheets that clouded a full moon. The lone streetlamp out front stood unlit.

The door creaked as we entered.

"That has to be her," Alexis whispered, pointing at the box from the doorway on our left. "The lights are off in the other room."

I nodded. We looked at each other, shuffling toward the gap between the coffin and its lid. We moved as one body, her left arm stuck to my right, neither one of us wanting to lose contact.

I stood at the head of the coffin and Alexis stood beside me. We put our fingertips in the gap and yanked the lid up.

SCREEEEEEEEEEEEEEEEEEEEEEEEEEEEEEEEEEEEEEEEKKKKKK!

I screamed.

The crash of the lid echoed off the folding chairs and rang in my ears.

Apparently, the hinges needed maintenance.

We stared at each other, mouths clenched, eyes bulging. She had her fingers over her mouth to keep from screaming.

We listened carefully for what seemed like minutes. The fluorescents overhead buzzed.

I slowly relaxed my hands, one clasped over my open mouth, the other clutching Alexis's arm.

"PPfffffffftttttt," I said, trying to hold in the giggles. Alexis stared at me, a smile playing around the edges of her mouth as I collapsed into laughter – great big belly laughs that in another person or lifetime would've been tearful sobs.

"You ready?" Alexis asked as I eventually calmed down.

"Oh! You still want – ?"

She nodded. Expecting the screeching hinges this time, we once again lifted the lid and let it rest against the back wall.

Michelle's skin was clear and smooth, the warm tint of a ripe peach in her cheeks. Peaceful. Asleep. The deepest of sleeps, where you want to wake your child in the middle of the night to make sure she's still breathing. I could imagine seeing her chest rise and fall with shallow breath.

Her dark brown curls framed her serene face. She wore her standard jeans and tee-shirt.

I expected her to open her dark brown eyes and grin at us, joking about how funny it was when the lid screeched, about how weird this all was, viewing a dead body.

"I don't see a wound," Alexis whispered.

"I don't know," I answered.

She nodded slightly, and we stared at each other for a moment, sharing our fascination and revulsion, all at once glad we'd missed the "official" viewing. They were going to play her favorite rock music. I imagined it blaring from the CD player while they cried.

Now that the laughter was out of my system, I felt angry, not understanding how she could have so little faith in the people around her, in her future, in hope. Remembering a time in my life a few years before when I'd considered doing the same thing, my conversation with Rod, and changing my mind.

"We should go," I said. We lowered the lid, gently this time.

A gray lady in tan orthopedic shoes met us at the door to the viewing room.

"Did you see all you needed?" she asked, her voice deep and scratchy from decades of smoking.

What an odd question, I thought.

"Yes," Alexis and I answered, and we headed out into the drab November rain.

## *Peggy*
### *2000–2001*

For about a year, I worked with a slight, soft-spoken counselor named Peggy. She came recommended to me by a good friend of mine during a particularly rough bout of depression that winter. I'd started my first teaching job in the fall and was finding it difficult to balance work with my marriage to Jeff.

At this point, Peggy and I were talking about a problem that concerned my mother's cats.

Yes, cats.

My mother and sister hadn't stayed an incredibly long time at my grandmother's house in California. They had, in fact, moved to an apartment about 10 miles from me almost the moment that my grandmother could take care of herself in the fall of 1994.

I was living in the dorm while in college when they moved to Portland, and as unbelievable as it seems now, I helped them move into their apartment. My sister was in high school at the time and had just moved into her third school in two years. I was hoping to make some of it, of everything, up to her, as impossible as that sounds.

I spent holidays with them, and my mother called me almost every day. These were the days before cell phones, so to find me she would call my dorm room, Jeff's apartment, and even one of the two or three jobs I was working to pay for school. Then she would talk about "bad news" – problems that I would be expected to solve, like when I was in the hospital after having Aaron and the dog had chewed up Jeff's softball glove.

Clearly, I was in survival mode. At this point in our entrenched relationship in the year 2000, my mother was out of town and my sister, who now had her own job and apartment, had agreed to take care of the cats. However, I lived closer to her apartment and my sister had decided that I should take over. I disagreed, but the codependence was kicking in pretty strong.

"What's the worst that could happen?" Peggy asked. She brought out a yellow pad and a pen.

"Well," I thought for a moment. "My sister will be mad."

"And?" Peggy handed the legal pad and pen to me, indicating I needed to write this down.

I wrote, at the top of the paper, "sister mad".

"My mom will be mad," I said, and wrote it down.

She nodded. "And?"

We went on like this for quite awhile. My list consisted of the following string of "the worst that could happen:"

- Sister mad
- Mom mad
- Sister and mom don't talk to me
- Silent treatment
- I end up alone
- I'm unloved
- My mom won't love me

We sat in silence for a bit as I soaked in this revelation.

"Do you think she loves you now?" Peggy asked.

The question cut me to my center. I knew the answer. I never did go back to seeing Peggy.

I never did feed the cats, either.

## The Absolute Right Thing
### Fall 2006

It took a surprisingly short amount of time to tell Hannah the series of events. I huddled in the oversized leather armchair under a fleece blanket. Used tissues and chocolate wrappers littered my lap.

"I wish I'd done something different, to stand up for myself somehow," I sobbed.

The questions that I'd asked a hundred times poured out of me.

Why didn't I tell someone? Why didn't I call the police? Why didn't I yell or scream? Why didn't I fight?

Why didn't I leave?

"You did what you knew was safe," Hannah said.

My sniffling filled the silence.

"You're a survivor!" Hannah said. "You did the absolute right thing. Who knows what would've happened if you had done something different."

The absolute right thing, I repeated to myself. The absolute right thing.

# SECTION FOUR

## The New Beginning

# 22

# When Can I Be Done With Grief?

## Dream #2 – No Shooting This Time
### August 2007

*I'M SITTING ON my dad's lap, as if he's Santa again like when I was a kid. I'm yelling at him, and as I do, I notice that my chest is growing bigger and bigger. I tap on it, and it's covered in a leathery armor, impenetrable.*

*"SEE, YOU CAN'T HURT ME!" I yell over and over, banging on the leathery shield.*

"Well, that's pretty clear," I said.

Hannah nodded.

"And less disturbing than the shotgun dream," I added.

## When Can I Be Done?
### September 2007

I perched in the overstuffed chair across from Hannah. I didn't want to be there. I didn't want to talk.

She was asking me questions, the answers to which I grunted noncommittally.

"Can I just be done?" I asked, interrupting her latest question.

"What do you mean?"

"When will I be done?" I leaned forward in my chair. "Isn't there a last step of some kind? There are stages of grief, right, that you pass through and then you're – well – DONE."

"What would it mean for you to be 'done'? What would have to happen?"

I sat in silence for several minutes, thinking.

"Whatcha thinkin' about?" Hannah asked.

"Justice."

"Have you considered that there might not be any justice?" Hannah asked quietly.

The truth of the statement hit me like a sledgehammer, shattering my denial and forcing me to admit the truth I'd known all along.

Tears welled up and overflowed onto my cheeks. I grabbed the box of tissue from the table next to me.

The truth was overwhelming.

There would never be any justice. A short mental list of injustices included:

- Lost innocence.
- Destroyed relationships.
- The cost of therapy, which wouldn't be reimbursed by my mother and father and with which I could potentially buy a small but reliable used car.
- No apology from either one of them. There would be no change of heart or radical behavioral transformations.
- Depression and PTSD as My Best Friends Forever.
- No punishment. Parents, friends, or relatives just as bad – or worse – than them continue to walk around and devastate children as if that's the norm.

There was, in fact, no justice.

I would never be done.

## Rules

*Rita reminded me of something I'd told her once, about the five rules of the world as arrived at by this Catholic priest named Tom Weston. The first rule, he says, is that you must not have anything wrong with you or anything different. The second one is that if you do have something wrong with you, you must get over it as soon as possible. The third rule is that if you can't get over it, you must pretend that you have. The fourth rule is that if you can't even pretend that you have, you shouldn't show up. You should stay home, because it's hard for everyone else to have you around. And the fifth rule is that if you're going to insist on showing up, you should at least have the decency to feel ashamed (100).*[2]

## *October 2007*

I sat at the counter on one of the wooden stools while Rachel scooped cookie dough onto metal sheets. Fresh, gooey, warm cookies cooled on wire racks, punctuated by melting chocolate chips.

For years, Rachel and I had made chocolate chip cookies during our visits. It had become our tradition, made even more enjoyable because we usually made cookies after the kids had gone to bed. We finally had time and space to formulate complete thoughts and sentences and really talk, like when we were in high school.

I sipped my tea while waiting for the cookies to cool. "So now," I continued, "I have to figure out what the specific Post-traumatic stress triggers are for me and then how to deal with them or avoid them all together. *AGH*, it's a lot to manage on top of everything else."

Rachel nodded, turning to put the cookie sheet in the oven. "You've been dealing with this stuff for a long time."

I nodded. "Yeah."

"When are you going to be done with it?"

I sat, too stunned to speak, trying to process her question.

Rachel looked at me, not a hint of animosity in her face, or any idea how much her question stabbed me in the chest.

How ironic.

Did I not just have this conversation with Hannah? I'd recently read the "Rules" by Anne Lamott in her book *Operating Instructions*, and I was apparently breaking all of the rules except for the fifth.

I refused to feel ashamed.

---

[2] Lamott, Anne. *Operating Instructions.* New York: First Anchor Book Edition, 2005.

"You know," I said. "I kind of get what you're saying. I want to be done, too – you know, put a check mark next to each stage and leave it behind." I paused. "In fact, I just talked to Hannah about it."

"What'd she say?" Rachel scooped dough onto the next cookie sheet in front of her. The stove timer counted down when the next cookies would be ready to come out.

"Doesn't work that way."

"Really?"

"Really."

Rachel nodded, walking into the living room. "What about a movie?"

"Sounds good," I said. I needed time to stare and process the conversation. To figure out how I felt about it, exactly. I was hurt by her question even as I understood it. Plus, in the space of a few comments, I was no longer sure of the friendship between Rachel and me.

Could I be friends with someone who wanted me to "get over" what would never be finished?

\* \* \*

"So are you still friends with Rachel?" Hannah asked.

Amazed at Rachel's question regarding when I would "be done," I'd opened the current counseling appointment by telling Hannah about it. I shrugged. "I don't really know."

"What did you think of her question?"

"The timing was entertaining, and I thought it was really ironic considering what Rachel's been through with Michelle."

"What do you mean?"

I pursed my lips, pausing to think for a moment. "Well, Rachel was different after Michelle died. I thought about it for awhile and came to the conclusion that there are just some things in life that forever change us."

"Okay," Hannah said, encouraging me to continue.

"There are some things that we just don't 'Get Over' or 'Get Through.' There are some things from which we can't come back."

Hannah nodded, pushing her glasses up while I faltered, trying to explain.

"And I don't think grief is in stages," I said.

"Really?"

"I think it's circular, or even spiral. I mean, take how I told you about myself over the years – starting from the end and circling back around. I think the stages of grief thing is fine, but as much as I might want it to, it doesn't work like that for me."

"How does it work?" she asked. She sat forward a little, leaning on the arm of the couch. I could almost see the wheels turning inside her head, and I knew she was with me.

I pointed an index finger at her and started moving it in a circle. "Like a spiral...like every time I come upon a new grief experience, there are echoes of the ones that came before."

I paused, and Hannah considered me for a moment. "Okay, I'm not supposed to say this," she said, "so you didn't hear it from me. But I think you're right."

"You're not 'supposed to say this'?" I asked. "Is there some kind of Grief Mafia that monitors your advice?"

She grinned. "No, not exactly. But...okay, let's not totally discount the stages of grief theory, but I think you're onto something."

# 23

## Crisis of Faith and Forgiveness

### *What Is Forgiveness, Exactly?*
### *December 2007*

**I WENT TO COLLEGE** in Portland beginning in August of 1993. My mother moved from California to an apartment about ten miles away the following year.

She called me almost every day. Sometimes multiple times a day. Unfortunately – in the days before cell phones – she would not only call my dorm room, she would call me at work.

How did I respond? I went to school full-time, studied, worked two jobs, and tried to get enough food and sleep. I tried to avoid her calls, screening them when I could. But I didn't shut her out of my life – there was this mysterious and unmistakable pull that she had over me, like I was a fish caught in a net.

Along with that feeling, I shoved everything that'd happened only a couple of years before into a small package and tied it tightly with a ribbon. Then I put it on a shelf in the back of my brain, locked in a closet. To mix metaphors even more, my job was to not rock the boat, and I did that job very well.

In the fall of 1993, I sat in my college sociology class, discussing the current social system that allows parents to regain custody of their kids after fulfilling certain obligations, like rehab or parenting classes. The discussion turned to whether or not this practice was the best for the children involved.

I'd been recently abandoned by my mother and father. I lived with my boyfriend's parents and worked a job in a fast-food restaurant while finishing my senior year of high school. When it came to paying college bills, I was on my own.

I felt I had a unique perspective. So I spoke up. "Absolutely not."

"Why not?" asked the professor.

"There's a bond that's been broken," I said. "And it cannot be repaired."

There are many ideas and philosophies I had in my late teens and early twenties that I now disagree with. But this idea – I think I was on to something.

There are just some things from which you can't come back.

It took me a long time to follow through with that idea, however. The clinching point came during an experience with my mother and sister at a busy highway truck stop in March of 2005.

We'd stopped for a short bathroom break – I was pregnant with Noah, my youngest child, at the time – during a long-distance road trip from a family reunion. It was eleven o'clock at night. Nobody else had to go, so I alone got out of the van, leaving two-year-old Aaron sleeping in his carseat.

I found the restroom and completed my business, and as the door to the women's bathroom shut behind me, I saw my mother and sister in line, buying cups of coffee and snacks for the road.

My son was still in the van. Alone. At a busy truck stop. The van's doors were unlocked.

When I got home, my husband and I made an appointment with a lawyer and had our wills drawn up. Should something happen to us, under no circumstances did I want my children in that…situation.

In December of 2007, I received some propaganda in the mail – in the form of a birthday card – from one of my aunts about forgiveness, with a thinly-veiled suggestion that I needed to forgive. What or whom I should forgive was mysteriously left unspoken, but I'd decided that I'd had enough, and wrote the following letter.

*   *   *

Mom,

*I received the attached document in my birthday card from Aunt Jean with no explanation for its purpose. I'm left to my own devices to guess why it was sent to me, and it seems to be directed to me in some way regarding forgiveness.*

*I can only assume that she's talking about my relationship with you. Our relationship has always been difficult for me considering the years of alcoholism and sexual abuse I endured.*

*What the attached document did was to help me discover what the Bible says regarding my situation. I found surprisingly little concerning incest – you can read about it in the Old Testament, Leviticus 18.*

*I've also believed for a while the idea that Grace requires a change of heart, which in one word is "repentance." When we accept Christ and enter into a relationship with him, aren't we expected to change our behavior to suit that decision?*

*Some of those behaviors include confession (I John 1:9), confronting and listening (Matt. 18:15-17), going from darkness to light/honesty (Acts 26:18) and changing our behavior with respect to the forgiveness we receive (Luke 17:3-4).*

*Since you were involved with my father for so long, I consider you partially responsible for my experiences. I don't see that you provided my sister or me any protection from him. You also let him back into our lives when Grandpa died, after you were divorced and had tried to help us get him prosecuted for sexual abuse. I questioned this at the time and received no explanation for your actions, or I received accusations that I "wouldn't understand."*

*It's traumatizing as a child to realize that your mother has chosen a violent, abusive man over you. As we've had a few (severely limited) conversations over the years, you've taken no responsibility for your choices or actions. There have been no apologies; there've only been excuses (There have been no apologies from my father either – I haven't received an apology or attempt at repentance or responsibility). There's been no confession or listening or honesty or change.*

*I feel like I've given this a lot of time. If any other person besides my parents had treated me so horribly, then I wouldn't be having a relationship with that person. And I don't think I would receive many questions about that decision. I've put off this decision because it's been so incredibly painful to deal with all of this the last year and a half.*

*Ironically, the attached document comes at a time when I'm questioning the nature of forgiveness. Fortunately, my dealings with God are intertwined in a relationship, and I know that He knows my heart. To give you an idea where I'm at in my spiritual life, I've included the testimony I gave at church Dec. 2nd.*

*So until I can figure more of this out for myself, I need to not have any contact with you. I can't do any visits or phone calls, and especially not Christmas. If you'd like to send gifts for the boys, that's fine; if not, that's also fine.*

*I'm giving myself until the summer time to re-evaluate what's next for me with regard to our relationship.*

\*    \*    \*

I read my mother's response to my letter only once. In spite of my request to not have contact, the envelope with neat but angry cursive arrived a few days after I'd sent mine.

I haven't ever been able to read it again. I remember highlights – I'm a bad mother, the many defenses of my father's actions so long ago as well as her own, and more than one accusation that I'm unforgiving.

More than once when we were on speaking terms, both of my parents stated that if I were a real Christian, then I would be more forgiving. And also, counseling doesn't and never will work. Which I think are two interesting ideas when you look at them side-by-side.

So if I choose not to have a relationship with my mother and father, does that mean I'm unforgiving?

During a Sunday morning sermon, the pastor of my church recently stated that, "Forgiveness costs, but unforgiveness costs more."

An unforgiving heart chooses to remain angry, to gossip, to complain about the situation. We believe we're entitled to our right to not forgive.

As I sat there mulling over the points of the sermon – and furiously taking notes – I came up with many questions. What role does forgiveness play in abusive situations? What does that even look like? Are there hurts and trauma experiences and actions that you just don't come back from? And if, as one of my friends says, "Grace requires a change of heart," why is it just my heart that changes? What about the other people involved?

After I received my mother's letter in response to mine, I knew for sure what needed to happen for my own welfare and that of my family. My mother says I'm unforgiving.

I disagree.

## Crisis of Faith Not Optional
### December 2, 2007

In 2006, I not only started my counseling appointments with Hannah, I also took that opportunity to question everything I believed spiritually up to that point in my life.

Yes, I became a Christian because Jesus and His talk of healing and abundant life looked quite good compared to my own experiences. But to be completely honest, I also really, really did not want to go to hell.

The whole idea of eternal suffering and Lake of Fire and demons scared the crap out of me, and I wanted what some (judgmental, maybe?) Christians call "Fire Insurance."

After wandering spiritually for a little while, I finally came to the conclusion that 1) I was having a crisis of faith and didn't know if I wanted to be a Christian anymore and 2) this process was not only okay, but should be required for all Christians everywhere. The questions that I was asking and the research I was completing regarding my beliefs – or lack thereof – in God meant that at least I was participating in my own spiritual growth.

It was during this process that the church I was attending at the time ran a series of sermons and study on healing. For a couple of Sundays in a row, there were testimonies by some of my church-mates regarding physical healing.

*Hold the phone. What about emotional and psychological healing?*

Wanting to be represented and believing that we don't talk enough about mental illness in our culture and especially in church, I brought this up with one of the pastors. In doing so, I knew that I was essentially volunteering to share my story the next Sunday in church, which is transcribed here:

> *I just turned thirty-three-years-old, which is significant to me since I remember thinking "WOW!" when I learned that Jesus was thirty-three when He died for us. First of all, I was fifteen at the time, so I thought thirty-three was really old and it would take a long time to reach. Conversely, I thought, that's just not a long life.*

> *I became a Christian when I was fifteen, about a year before my family imploded from years of abuse and alcoholism. I attended Olympia-Lacey Church of God at the time, and I owe them a great deal for being a surrogate family. Left on my own, I lived with another family my senior year of high school and determined to go to college.*

> *It was during this time when I asked a few questions – not too many – about my situation. I was a new Christian in a precarious place in my life. All I asked about my situation was, "OK, why would my parents treat me so terribly?" The reasonable answers were, "It's a fallen world," and "Unfortunately we pay the price for other people's sin." I accepted these answers – I needed to survive.*

> *I worked my way through college (God sent me to Warner Pacific) and since counseling services at the college were free, I took advantage of them. I decided then that I wouldn't be*

*like my family – I would live differently, calling on the abundant life that God promises in Scripture. So I shoved my experiences with sexual abuse and pain and betrayal into a box, much like shoving too much into a suitcase (which I do regularly). I wrapped a ribbon around it and set it far back on a shelf in my brain. Far, far back on that shelf.*

*It collected dust there until about five years ago, when my oldest son was born, and we both almost died. On the same day, a good friend of mine had a baby, and her baby died. And the box thumped its way toward the front of my brain, and the ribbons strained. And "It's a fallen world" wasn't doing it for me anymore.*

*I didn't know if I wanted to be a Christian anymore. I had a lot of questions, and now, at a safer time in my life, I could ask them. I was angry enough to not be afraid to ask God, "Why did I live? Why did Aaron live? Why did my friend's baby die? Why her and not me?"*

*Aaron was born ten weeks early, so he had an extended stay in the NICU. During this time, which I considered one of the worst in my life, people would say to me, "You're so blessed." And I asked, "Is this true?" Because I didn't feel blessed; I felt despair; what about my friend whose baby died? Was she also blessed? I asked, "Does God choose, and if He does, then how?" and "What is suffering?" And I didn't have any answers to my questions.*

*When I was pregnant with my second son, I spent a month in the hospital, where at any moment, he could sit on his umbilical cord and die. At this point, quite frankly, it was my opinion that I'd been through enough in my life. Impatient for answers now, I asked, "What's the deal?" And my tone was harsh. The box bulged and thumped.*

*And Noah didn't die, but was born only seven weeks early, so his stay in the NICU was much shorter. And my postpartum depression was pretty bad. And the box, with my pain and suffering and questions, wouldn't stay closed any more. It was time to live the healing process I'd heard so much about.*

*I've been digging around in that box, with help, for the last year and a half. There've been times that I thought I would be crushed by the pain. I've worried that I would drown in my own tears. I've agonized over being a good wife and mother. And I've also worried about being a good Christian.*

*I'm thirty-three now. In "Christian" years I'm eighteen, but I know that God will not push me out of the nest, so to speak. I still ask a lot of questions – Who is God? Does He really love me? Do I want to be a Christian?*

*I do. Because through all of this grief and pain, through this frightening world and life, I have found Hope. Hope with God, through Scripture. Hope with God's people, who encourage me to keep standing, and who have as many questions as I do.*

*If you haven't yet, I encourage you to ask those tough questions. Present God with the ones you're afraid to ask. Let's embrace this process of healing instead of fighting against it. And the question I'm wondering now is, isn't it the nature of faith to ask questions, to live with uncertainty instead of fighting against it?*

# 24

# New Beginnings

### It's All in the Breeding
### November 2008

**"BUT WHAT IF I** turn out just like her?" I asked. "What if I'm just like them?"

"Like your mom?" Hannah asked.

I nodded. "Both. Mom and Dad."

"Impossible."

"Why? How can you be so sure?"

"Breeding," she said in a matter-of-fact tone.

"What're you talking about?"

"Don't you know about the one-in-four-breeding-principle?" she asked. She said it as if the five words were all one.

I shook my head.

"Oh, well," she continued eagerly, "this is exciting. When two genetically weak animals are bred, there's a one in four chance that their offspring will be genetically exceptional in some way."

I stared at her, disbelieving. This was way out of my sphere of experience. Or general belief.

"Exceptional how?" I asked.

"Physically, athletically, intelligence, stuff like that," she answered. "You had siblings, right?"

"A sister."

"Now think about if there had been four children instead of two." Hannah spread her hands wide. "You're the one in four."

I had to laugh. I'll take what I can get.

## New Beginnings
### November/December 2008

I trolled the aisles of the fabric store, shopping for bargains, as I often do. Autumn decorations were now at least half off, if not more – cute "Happy Harvest" signs for the front door or my living room mantle, wreaths of silk leaves in various hues, and cute scarecrows winking at me.

I already had enough autumn decorations since it was my favorite time of year. But still, I loved a good bargain.

I turned a corner to peruse the items in the next aisle and stopped short.

Christmas stuff.

My heart skipped, and I glanced around in confusion. I felt something in my chest, but it wasn't panic or heartburn from the Mexican food I'd eaten at lunch.

I remembered Jeff in the Santa mask years before and the PTSD and the sweating and the shaking. This feeling wasn't like that at all.

I felt something, but it was different somehow. It was an emotion, familiar yet unrecognizable when combined with the idea of Christmas.

Excitement.

I stood, stunned, thinking about how last Christmas my six-year-old helped me frost sugar cookies and my three-year-old picked out his favorite Christmas tree ornament. I thought about how their sweet faces lit up at the sight of falling snow, and how the Christmas holidays could hold joy instead of grief and sorrow.

Excitement. About Christmas.

*   *   *

The following Sunday morning, one of the pastors of my church gave a sermon in which she began with this statement, "Christmas is a time for new beginnings."

I had to smile.

Here's to new beginnings.

# ABOUT THE AUTHOR

Kelly Wilson is an author and comedian who entertains and inspires with stories of humor, healing, and hope. As a survivor of childhood sexual abuse, Kelly writes and speaks about finding hope in the process of recovery. Through both stand-up and improv comedy, she brings laughter to audiences of all ages using a wide range of subject matter, including silly songs, parenting stories, and jokes and anecdotes revolving around mental health issues.

Kelly is the author of *Live Cheap & Free, Don't Punch People in the Junk*, and *Caskets From Costco*, along with numerous articles and short stories for children and adults. She currently writes for a living and lives with her Magically Delicious husband, junk-punching children, dog, cat, and stereotypical minivan in Portland, Oregon. Read more about Kelly and her work at www.wilsonwrites.com.

Made in the USA
San Bernardino, CA
04 May 2019